Academic Writer's Guide to Periodicals, Vol. III

African

and

Black American Studies

Academic Writer's Guide to Periodicals, Vol. III

COMPILED AND EDITED BY

lexander S. Birkos

rmerly Managing Editor
storical Abstracts

Lewis A. Tambs

Director, Center for Latin
American Studies,
Arizona State University

1975

LIBRARIES UNLIMITED, INC.

Littleton, Colo.

LIBRARIES UNLIMITED, INC.
P.O. Box 263
Littleton, Colorado 80120

Library of Congress Cataloging in Publication Data

Birkos, Alexander S
  African and Black American studies.

  (Academic writer's guide to periodicals ; v. 3)
  Includes indexes.
  1. Africa--Periodicals--Bibliography. 2. Negroes--
Periodicals--Bibliography. 3. Negro race--Periodicals
--Bibliography. I. Tambs, Lewis A., 1927-   joint
author. II. Title. III. Series.
Z3503.B57   016.30145'19'6   74-31262
ISBN 0-87287-109-6

TABLE OF CONTENTS

To

Dr. Donald Marquand Dozer,

scholar, mentor, and friend.

L.A.T.

PREFACE

The decade of the 1970s promises to be a dynamic one for writers in the humanities and social sciences. New ideas, fresh concepts, and innovative approaches are emerging concurrently with an ever-growing number of new periodicals. Never before has the scholar had as many outlets, or as much competition, for the publication of articles. Many types of periodicals are available to the writer and the student—from the popular ones with wide appeal to the deeply specialized, highly scholarly journals.

Journals will continue to function as the professional medium of communication within the academic community. This guide is designed not only to support and serve the producing scholar of today but to stimulate and sharpen the specialist of tomorrow.

A.S.B.

L.A.T.

ACKNOWLEDGMENTS

The compilers would like to thank the numerous journal editors who were kind enough to cooperate in the preparation of this *Guide*. We appreciate their taking time from their busy hours to answer our many questions; without their assistance this publication would not have been possible.

We wish once again to acknowledge a debt of gratitude to Dr. Paul G. Hubbard, Associate Dean of the College of Liberal Arts, Arizona State University, for his splendid support. Mr. Joseph Holtey and Mr. Lowell Williams of the Department of History were also most helpful. Special mention must go, however, to the staff of the Center for Latin American Studies, Mrs. Katharine Phillips, Miss Randi LeGendre, and Miss Lorraine Anderson. Miss Anderson's contribution, in particular, was outstanding. Mr. Elliot Palais, Reference Coordinator of the Hayden Library, continued to give us his expert professional help and guidance.

Professor Bruce Mason, Department of Political Science, Arizona State University, augmented our selection of African journals, and Mr. Robert N. Nesby, Department of History, brought numerous Black-American periodicals to our attention.

Dr. Bohdan S. Wynar of Libraries Unlimited patiently handled our many queries and missives.

The responsibility for any errors lies with the compilers alone.

A.S.B.
L.A.T.

INTRODUCTION

The English-speaking academic community in the humanities and social sciences has expanded tremendously since the end of World War II. There has also been a proportionate increase in the number of periodicals in these disciplines. This tandem growth has resulted in a torrent of published research. Each year sees the establishment of journals catering to both specialized and generalized academic interests. Moreover, new periodicals continually appear in response to fresh trends or forces on the contemporary scene—as illustrated by such publications as *Second Order*, which concentrates on the growing awareness and worth of African philosophy; *Journal of Developing Areas*, which covers the whole range of problems connected with man's development; and *Zambian Urban Studies*, which reflects new concern for urban problems. To date, however, little effort has been made to provide the academic writer with a guide to the subject interest and editorial policies of the hundreds of journals extant in the humanities and social sciences. This guide seeks to fill that need.

The *Academic Writer's Guide to Periodicals* is a projected multi-volume area study series covering periodicals devoted to the disciplines within the humanities and social sciences. The first two volumes, published by Kent State University Press, covered Latin American and Soviet/East European studies. Future volumes will cover Middle Eastern, Asian and Pacific, West European and Scandinavian, and American and Canadian studies.

SCOPE AND METHOD

This volume, devoted to African and Black American studies, concentrates on periodicals and monograph series that publish at least a portion of their articles in the English language. In a few cases, journals that do not publish in English but that do accept or consider English-language manuscripts have been included in this *Guide*. Also noted, for the benefit of those writers whose basic language is other than English, are periodicals that accept manuscripts in other languages. The compilers have made an extra effort to ascertain whether or not African and Black American journals accept manuscripts and publish solely in English and, contrary to the *Guide*'s standard practice, have indicated such a policy in the entry.

This *Guide* to African and Black American studies focuses on serial publications with either a primary or an occasional interest in any of the areas of Africa (North, Central, South, East, or West), the African nations of the Middle East, or the nations or colonies on the African continent. Included also are publications that deal with Black American interests in Canada, Latin America, and the United States.

11

The data for each periodical were obtained by means of questionnaires sent to hundreds of journals all over the world. The completeness or brevity of any given entry is directly related to the editor's response.

The compilers have tried to provide up-to-date information on the journals compiled. However, the present inflationary spiral of prices and the weakness of United States currency have affected publication costs, and numerous journals may have increased their subscription rates after this manuscript went to press.

An interesting, and possibly alarming, side effect of inflation is reflected in the rising number of journals that request potential authors to pay a submission fee. This initial subvention, while justified in order to compensate referees adequately, may tend to discourage offerings from graduate students or from faculty at less well endowed institutions of higher learning.

ORGANIZATION

The entries are arranged alphabetically by title. If a periodical carries its title in several languages, the English-language title was preferred.

Sample Journal Entry

PHOENIX: Afro-American Studies on War and Peace[1]

Editor: J. John Smith[2]

Editorial address:
    311 Camden Way
    Center City, Anystate 00001

Sponsor: Institute of Advanced African Studies[3]

Frequency: Q   Founded: 1974
Subscription: $12 individual,   Subscribers: 8,000[4]
    $15 institutional

Editorial interest:[5]
    Chronological: 1492 to present
    Geographical: Africa, United States, West Indies
    Topical: unrestricted[6]
    Special scope: the dysfunction and development of society during war
        and peace[7]

Editorial policies:
    Query prior to submission of ms.[8]
    Style manual: Chicago;[9] "Contributor's Guidance Sheet" is available on
        request[10]
    Preferred length of ms.: 8,000-10,000 words;[11] longer articles for
        serialization occasionally accepted[12]
    Author payment:[13] $75-$150, 3 copies of issue in which article appears,
        and 25 article reprints.

PHOENIX (cont'd)

Bottom notes.[14] Potential authors must be past or present members of the Institute.[15] Accepts Arabic-, East African-, French-, German-, Italian-, and Spanish-language mss.;[16] publishes articles in English.[17] Articles must be of interest to an international audience of historians.[18] Wants articles that deal with new approaches to interdisciplinary or comparative historical studies.[19]

Notes: Articles abstracted in *African Abstracts*, HA.[20]

Special features:[21] listings of manuscript collections in the United States and Africa. Authors should submit two copies of ms. and a 200-word English-language abstract.[22] Book reviews are assigned, but occasional free-lance offerings are accepted; no remuneration.[23] Reports on mss. in one to two months.[24]

EXPLANATORY NOTES TO SAMPLE ENTRY

1. Subtitles are included.
2. Titles and names of chief editorial personnel.
3. Title of group or institution that sponsors a given journal.
4. Number of paid subscribers. Term *circulation* denotes either free or partially free distribution.
5. Indicates the subject areas of interest for a periodical.
6. Term *unrestricted* indicates that a periodical does not limit its sphere of interest to a certain area.
7. The special scope statement identifies a particular area or theme of editorial interest.
8. In some cases a journal will not accept a manuscript unless approval has been given in previous correspondence with an author.
9. In some cases a periodical prescribes a particular manual of style for prospective authors for the preparation of manuscripts, in this case *A Manual of Style* (University of Chicago Press, 12th edition).
10. Some periodicals have their own style guidance sheets giving specific requirements for the preparation of mss.
11. The preferred length of a manuscript is given either in number of words or in number of typed pages.
12. Indicates that articles of substantial length are occasionally accepted for publication in two or more parts.
13. Kind and amount of payment for articles.
14. "Bottom notes" indicates that reference notes are to be typed at the bottom of relevant text pages. "End notes" indicates that notes are to be typed on separate pages after the last page of text. "No notes" indicates that a journal does not require reference notes for its articles.
15. Indicates that manuscripts are accepted only from a certain group of individuals.
16. Identifies in what language manuscripts may be submitted (in addition to English).

17. The languages in which that journal publishes.

18. Describes the kind and level of readership audience.

19. The kinds of articles that are particularly encouraged for submission.

20. Indication of which reference publications abstract, cite, or index the journal's articles. *African Abstracts* suspended publication in 1974; however, it is cited in order to aid researchers seeking information in previous issues. *SSHI—Social Sciences and Humanities Index*—was divided into two parts, *Social Sciences Index* and *Humanities Index*, beginning June 1974. Future editions of *Academic Writer's Guide to Periodicals* will designate in which of these two sections a journal is carried.

21. Recurring features, other than articles and book reviews, of a periodical that may have some value for scholars but that are not usually cited in reference publications.

22. Additional statements regarding ms. preparation or submission.

23. Statement on the book review policies of a periodical; "no remuneration" indicates that no cash payment is made for book reviews.

24. Indication as to length of time the editorial staff needs before making a decision on a submitted article.

INDEXES

The user of this guide can quickly locate the journals that fall within his chronological, geographical, and/or topical interests by consulting the analytical indexes. The journals that have no limitations upon any of these parameters of editorial interest are listed in the sub-category "Unrestricted."

Some journals listed in the indexes are marked with an asterisk (*). This signifies that particular attention should be given to qualifying remarks in the main entry concerning editorial interests. For example, while *African Social Research* has no restrictions on the chronological or topical range, the notation in the main entry indicates that articles must focus on human problems in Central Africa. In this instance, the writer is well advised to study the journal and to send a query letter with a 200-word summary of a proposed article, as the editor requests, before submitting a complete manuscript.

The topical index covers broad subject areas only. Anyone interested in Pan-Africanism, for example, should determine what broader subject field encompasses his area of specialty—e.g., economics, literature, sociology—and then search under that category. Thus, the writer who concentrates upon the literary aspects of Pan-Africanism should consult the literature subdivision of the topical index to find which journals might be potential outlets for his work.

SUGGESTIONS FOR MANUSCRIPT
PREPARATION AND SUBMISSION

In the course of compiling data for this *Guide*, serial editors were asked to suggest ways in which potential contributors could increase their chances of publication. From many of the comments offered there emerged a number of general principles. These suggestions are similar to those found in many guides for professional freelance writers.

The aspiring academic writer should first list those journals that seem likely as publishing outlets for an article, completed or projected. He then should take the time to read and study a few successive issues of each of those periodicals in order to ascertain what kinds of articles are published. This reading prior to the submission of a manuscript or query letter will enable the author to acquaint himself with a periodical's style, scope, audience focus, and discernible biases, if any. Such reading will also quickly show that no two periodicals, even in the same specialized field, are alike in editorial tastes and requirements. The writer, therefore, must decide whether his article actually addresses itself to the audience of a particular journal. If it does not fit into the focus of one periodical, the author should then check other journals. What may not be welcomed by one editor is often eagerly sought and received by another.

The author should next determine whether the journal requires a letter of inquiry before submission of a completed manuscript; this information is found in the "Editorial Policies" section of the main entry for that journal. Some editors will not consider unsolicited manuscripts unless they have first received a letter indicating the chronological, geographical, and topical parameters of a projected article, the approximate length, and an indication as to the use of illustrated materials. The query letter should be concise, never more than one page in length, and should state the significance or main thesis of the projected article. From such query letters editors can often ascertain beforehand whether the material will fit into their publications, thus saving their own time as well as the author's. Naturally, courtesy dictates that the author send a stamped, self-addressed envelope with the query letter.

There are hundreds of possible outlets for article-length manuscripts. This *Guide* should help an author to find not one, but several, journals that might be interested in publishing his manuscript. However, only one editor at a time should be contacted about an article. Multiple simultaneous submissions of the same manuscript to different editors is not only unethical but embarrassing, should the writer receive multiple acceptances, and it could give the author an unfavorable reputation among editors.

If a query letter is neither required nor advised, the writer is, of course, free to submit an unsolicited manuscript. Before doing so, however, he should check the manuscript carefully to insure that it conforms to the style prescribed for that periodical. In many cases journals have style guidance sheets that will be sent on request to potential contributors. A manuscript must adhere to the prescribed style because no editor has the time or staff to revise or recast articles that obviously do not meet his journal's style requirements. In many instances articles are rejected for this reason alone. Whenever possible, it is strongly recommended that the writer request these style sheets. They indicate the desired length of a manuscript, illustrate the form for reference notes and bibliographies, and occasionally provide instructions for the preparation of illustrative or graphic materials. Some style sheets also provide extensive information regarding a journal's thematic interests, which can illustrate or indicate areas for possible future research and also provide some insight to the reading audience.

Trite as it may sound, clarity of expression and simplicity in the choice of words are hallmarks of good writing.* Every writer, in revising and rewriting his or her work, must constantly ask himself if he is saying what he really wants to say in such a way that the reader will have no doubts as to the meaning. Clear, simple language with a modicum of jargon—if necessary at all—is indeed what most editors want, because it eases the communication and comprehension of ideas. Excellence in writing is not usually easy to come by; it requires much time, study, and practice. Nevertheless, it should be the objective of all writers for, as G. K. Chesterton remarked, "good literature tells us about the subject matter, bad literature about the author."

Any writer who wishes to win an editor's favorable attention has to attend to the mechanics of writing. Correct spelling, grammar, punctuation, and appropriateness in word selection are all essential elements of the writer's craft (in addition to competence in the subject matter itself). Each writer should keep close at hand a dictionary, a thesaurus, and a manual of style.

The final version of the manuscript is always typewritten—never handwritten—on 8½ x 11-inch, white, unlined bond paper of good quality. Everything must be typed *double-spaced*, including reference notes and bibliography, and on one side of the page only. The final copy should be clean and as error-free as possible. Only the original copy is sent to an editor, except in cases where editors request a second or third copy to expedite editorial evaluation. Margins should be at least 1½ inches; some editors require 2-inch margins.

---

*See Theodore M. Bernstein, *The Careful Writer* (New York: Atheneum, 1968), for a humorous and pointed example of "windyfoggery" (pp. 480-82), and H. W. Fowler, *A Dictionary of Modern English Usage* (New York: Oxford University Press, 1965), for an example of "abstractitis" (pp. 5-6) and for an example of "pedantic humour" (p. 441).

At the upper right hand corner of the first page there should be an indication of the approximate number of words in the manuscript. The word count is calculated by multiplying the number of words on a full page of text by the number of pages. The author's name and mailing address should be typed at the upper left hand corner of the first page; some editors, however, prefer to have no indication of the writer's name anywhere on the manuscript except on a cover sheet—a point usually covered in the journals' guidance sheets. Page numbers are to be typed, after the first page of the manuscript, in the upper right hand corner following an abbreviated title of the article.

The manuscript should be mailed (by first class or special fourth class-manuscript rate) flat and unbound in a 9 x 12-inch envelope, along with a stamped, self-addressed return envelope. If the manuscript is being sent to a foreign journal, a check or International Reply Coupon should be sent to cover return postage. Editors are not responsible for the return of manuscripts unless the writer provides a return envelope with sufficient postage. The author should always retain a copy of the manuscript before mailing the original. This is to insure against loss if the original is misrouted or lost in the mails.

An author can expect to wait about three to eight weeks before receiving either a letter acknowledging receipt of the manuscript or an editor's decision. If no answer is received after eight weeks, a letter of inquiry regarding the manuscript should be sent to the editor. It is the writer's responsibility to keep track of his manuscript.

The foregoing remarks do not in any way constitute a certain path to publication, but they do represent some long-standing conventions which, if scrupulously observed, lead to having manuscripts received with an approving eye by editors.

KEY TO ABBREVIATIONS AND SYMBOLS

AA	*Abstracts in Anthropology*
AES	*Abstracts of English Studies*
AFS	*Abstracts of Folklore Studies*
AHL	*America: History and Life*
AI	*Agricultural Index*
APS	*Advance Bibliography of Contents: Political Science and Government*
AULI	*Air University Library Index to Military Periodicals*
BHM	*Bibliography of the History of Medicine*
BPI	*Business Periodicals Index*
CC	*Current Contents: Behavioral, Social and Management Sciences*
Chicago	*A Manual of Style* (University of Chicago Press)
CPI	*Catholic Periodicals Index*
EI	*Education Index*
Engr I	*Engineering Index*
HA	*Historical Abstracts*
HLAS	*Handbook of Latin American Studies*
IJP	*Index to Jewish Periodicals*
ILP	*Index to Legal Periodicals*
IPAL	*Index to Periodical Articles Related to Law*
IPSA	*International Political Science Abstracts*
IRPL	*Index to Religious Periodical Literature*
JEL	*Journal of Economic Literature*
LLBA	*Language and Language Behavior Abstracts*
MLA	Modern Language Association
ms(s).	manuscript(s)
PA	*Psychological Abstracts*

PAIS	*Public Affairs Information Service Bulletin*
Phil I	*Philosopher's Index*
PI	*Population Index*
PMLA	*Publications of the Modern Language Association*
PRA	*Peace Research Abstracts Journal*
RGPL	*Reader's Guide to Periodical Literature*
RTA	*Religious and Theological Abstracts*
SA	*Sociological Abstracts*
SSHI	*Social Sciences and Humanities Index**
USGPO	*U.S. Government Printing Office Style Manual*

**SSHI was divided into two parts, *Social Sciences Index* and *Humanities Index*, beginning June 1974.

ABBREVIATIONS FOR
FREQUENCY OF PUBLICATION

A	Annually
B	Biennially
BM	Bimonthly
BW	Biweekly
M	Monthly
Q	Quarterly
SA	Semiannually
TA	Triannually
W	Weekly
xy	times per year
irr	irregular

SYMBOLS FOR CURRENCY

A$	Australian dollars
BeFr	Belgian francs
CFr	Congo francs
Cr$	Brazilian cruzeiros
d	pence (United Kingdom)
Dcr	Danish crowns
Dfl	Dutch guilders
Din	Yugoslav dinars
Dj	Jordanian dinars
DM	Deutsch marks (West Germany)
$	dollars (United States)
Fr	francs (France)
Ft	Hungarian forints
HK$	Hong Kong dollars
ID	Tunisian, Iraqi dinars
IL	Israeli pounds
Kcs	Czechoslovak crowns
L	Italian lira
£	pounds sterling (United Kingdom)
Ncr	Norwegian crowns
NL	Nigerian pounds
PRs	Pakistan rupees
ptas	pesetas
Rds	South African rands
Rs	Indian, Ceylon rupees
S	Austrian shillings
s	shillings (United Kingdom)

Scr	Swedish crowns
Sfr	Swiss francs
Y	Japanese yen

Compilers' note: The prices for annual subscription rates were provided by the editors of the journals surveyed. Because of fluctuating exchange rates, the compilers have not attempted to give U.S.$ equivalents in cases where only foreign currencies were cited.

PERIODICAL LISTING

ABERDEEN UNIVERSITY AFRICAN STUDIES GROUP BULLETIN

Editor: R. C. Bridges

Editorial address:
Department of History
King's College
Aberdeen AB9 2UB, Scotland

Sponsor: Aberdeen University African Studies Group

Frequency: irr.; at least one issue per year
Subscription: £0.50, or exchange; free
    to members

Founded: 1967
Subscribers: 88, distribution
    275

Editorial interest:
Chronological: unrestricted
Geographical: Africa
Topical: unrestricted

Editorial policies:
A staff-written newsletter that records the activities and interests of those at Aberdeen interested in African studies.

Notes:
Special features: Bibliographical information on Aberdeen's SCOLMA Area of Africa (Chad, Gabon, Central African Republic, Cameroon, and Congo-Brazzaville)

AFER: African Ecclesiastical Review

Editor: J. Geerdes

Editorial address:
P.O. Box 232
Masaka, Uganda

Sponsor: AMECA (Association of Members of Episcopal Conferences of Eastern Africa)

Frequency: Q
Subscription: 20 East African shillings in
    Africa; 25 East African shillings elsewhere

Founded: 1958
Subscribers: 1,800

AFER (cont'd)

Editorial interest:

Chronological: unrestricted

Geographical: Africa

Topical: anthropology, art, church or ecclesiastical affairs, cultural
affairs, education, ethnology, philosophy, religious studies

Editorial policies:

Query prior to submission of ms.

Style manual: none prescribed

Preferred length of ms.: 4,000 words, longer articles for serialization
occasionally considered.

Author payment: 60 East African shillings and 20 article reprints.

Accepts mss. and publishes articles in English. Wants mss. that contribute
to the growth of Christianity in Africa.

Notes: Articles abstracted or cited in *Bibliographia Missionaria* (Rome),
Cannon Law Abstracts (Edinburgh), *Eglise Vivante* (Louvain). Book
reviews are solicited; no remuneration. Persons interested in reviewing
should contact the editor.

AFRICA: Journal of the African Institute

Editor: Prof. J. Middleton

Assistant editor: Barbara Pym

Editorial address:

International African Institute

St. Dunstan's Chambers

10-11 Fetter Lane, Fleet Street

London EC4A 1BJ, England

Sponsor: same as above

Frequency: Q   Founded: 1928

Subscription: £4 individual, £5 institutional   Subscribers: 2,700

Editorial interest:

Chronological: unrestricted

Geographical: Africa

Topical: anthropology, art, ethnology, folklore, language (philology,
semantics), religious studies, social history, sociology

Special scope: linguistics

Editorial policies:

Style manual: own house style printed in each issue; also accepts style
of *American Anthropologist*

Preferred length of ms.: 8,000 words maximum including notes and
references; longer articles for serialization occasionally accepted
if subvention provided to cover extra printing costs

Author payment: 25 article reprints

Bottom or end notes. Accepts mss. and publishes articles in English, French, and occasionally German. Potential authors should write for scholars in African anthropology, sociology, and linguistics. Mss. must be scholarly and of the highest quality.

Notes: Articles abstracted in *African Abstracts*, HA

Special features: "News and Notes" on research, conferences, publications, etc. Potential authors are urged to consult previous issues. Book reviews are assigned, but freelance offerings are occasionally accepted; small fee remuneration if reviewer declines to retain book.

AFRICA INSTITUTE BULLETIN

Editor: C. F. de Villiers

Editorial address:
P.O. Box 630
Pretoria, South Africa

Sponsor: Africa Institute of South Africa

Frequency: 10 xy	Founded: 1963
Subscription: Rds 4.80/$6.72	Subscribers: 8,000

Editorial interest:
Chronological: current events
Geographical: Africa
Topical: agriculture, anthropology, business, communications media, cultural affairs, demography, economics, education, ethnology, foreign relations, geography, military affairs, politics and government, religious studies, social history
Special scope: external powers' relationships with African countries

Editorial policies:
Query letter preferred, but not necessary
Style manual: *Oxford English Dictionary* and H. W. Fowler, *A Dictionary of Modern English Usage*
Preferred length of ms.: 10-20 typed pages; serialization in exceptional cases
Author payment: varies according to assessed value of article, can be negotiated prior to final acceptance of ms.; six copies of issue in which article appears
End notes. Accepts mss. and publishes articles in Afrikaans or English, but will consider mss. in other languages for translation if article is exceptional. Potential contributors should write for a worldwide audience interested in gaining and promoting a greater understanding of and among the peoples of Africa. Wants mss. on contemporary history, current socio-economic trends, developments, and prospects which contain background information on modern

Africa. The editors are not interested in promoting political
ideologies, but in creating better understanding of and among the
peoples of Africa.

Notes: Indexed in SSHI

Special features: "Spotlight," which presents news on economic
developments not normally published in the popular press, and
studies on individual African countries in concise but comprehen-
sive form. Book reviews are solicited; no remuneration. Editorial
decision on submissions in one month.

**AFRICA MAGAZINE: An International Business, Economic and Political
Monthly**

Editor-in-chief: Raph Uwechue

Editorial address:
51 Avenue des Terbes
Paris 17ème, France

Sponsor: Jeune Afrique

Frequency: M	Founded: 1971
Subscription: $10	Subscribers: approximately 1,000

Editorial interest:
Chronological: current events
Geographical: Africa (mainly), Latin America, and Black areas of United
States, West Indies
Topical: agriculture, business, cultural affairs, economics, education,
ethnology, foreign relations, international organizations, legal
and constitutional affairs, military affairs, politics and government,
research methods, science and technology
Special scope: the Black World

Editorial policies:
Query prior to submission of ms.
Style manual: consult previous issues
Preferred length of ms.: 800-1,000 words, or longer when agreed. In the
latter case the article is signed. Longer articles for serialization
are accepted by previous agreement only.
Author payment: £20 for 800 words, £25 for 1,000 words, £30 for
1,500 words, etc.; complimentary copies of issue in which article
appears by previous arrangement.
Bottom or end notes. Accepts mss. and publishes articles in English.
Address mss. to the editor-in-chief. Potential authors should
write for a "public mainly African which is interested in political
and economic affairs regarding the African continent." Wants mss.
that are "detailed and well thought out on politics, economics,
education, development and business in individual African countries."

AFRICA MAGAZINE (cont'd)

Notes:

Special features: "Africans Overseas" and interviews with prominent Africans. Freelance book reviews are considered if they deal with the African scene or the Black World; remuneration at the same rates as for articles. Editorial reports on submissions within one month. Illustrated.

AFRICA REPORT

Editor: Anthony J. Hughes

Editorial address:
833 United Nations Plaza
New York, New York 10017

Sponsor: African-American Institute

Frequency: BM
Subscription: $9

Founded: 1956
Circulation: 12,000

Editorial interest:
Chronological: unrestricted
Geographical: Africa
Topical: unrestricted

Editorial policies:
Query prior to submission of ms.
Style manual: none prescribed
Preferred length of ms.: 2,500-3,500 words; longer articles accepted for serialization
Author payment: $25-$100, and some article reprints.
No reference notes. Accepts mss. in any modern language. Publishes articles in English.

Notes: Book reviews are assigned; no remuneration

AFRICA RESEARCH BULLETIN
Political, Social and Cultural Series—A
Economic, Financial and Technological Series—B

Editor: W. M. Dickenson

Editorial address:
1 Parliament Street
Exeter,
Devon EX1 1AA, England

Frequency: M, each series
Subscription: Series A, £20/$52 surface, £21/$54.50 air; Series B, £33.50/$87 surface, £34.50/$90 air; combined Series A and B, £46/$119.50 surface, £48.50/$126 air.

Founded: 1964
Subscribers: approximately 1,500

AFRICA RESEARCH BULLETIN (cont'd)

Editorial interest:
 Chronological: current events
 Geographical: Africa
 Topical: unrestricted

Editorial policies:
 Query prior to submission of ms., since outside articles are not
  generally accepted
 Style manual: none prescribed
 Preferred length of ms.: unspecified
 Author payment: one copy of issue in which article appears
 No reference notes. Accepts English- and French-language mss. Publishes
  in English.

Notes: Staff-written general coverage of significant events affecting Africa or
 events inside Africa. Maps.

AFRICA TODAY

Editors: Tilden LeMelle, Ezekiel Mphahlele, and George Shepherd, Jr.

Executive editor: Edward A. Hawley

Editorial address:
 Africa Today Associates
 Graduate School of International Relations
 University of Denver
 University Park Campus
 Denver, Colorado 80210

Sponsor: same as above

Frequency: Q   Founded: 1954
Subscription: $8 individual; $12 institutional   Subscribers: 3,000

Editorial interest:
 Chronological: 1900 to present
 Geographical: Africa
 Topical: art, bibliographical articles, church or ecclesiastical affairs,
  cultural affairs, economics, education, foreign relations, literature
  (history and criticism), politics and government, social history,
  sociology
 Special scope: United States-African relations, poetry

Editorial policies:
 Query prior to submission of ms. optional
 Style manual: Kate L. Turabian, *A Manual for Writers*
 Preferred length of ms.: 8-10 typed pages; might consider longer articles
  for serialization
 Author payment: five article reprints
 Bottom or end notes. Accepts mss. and publishes articles in English.

AFRICA TODAY (cont'd)

Potential authors should write for "persons with some scholarly interest in general awareness of African problems."

Notes: Articles abstracted in AHL, CARDAN (Paris), HA, PAIS
Special features: current political assessments, list of publications on Africa. Book reviews are normally solicited, but freelance offerings are considered. No remuneration. Those interested in book reviewing should write the executive editor. Editorial reports on submissions in three months maximum.

AFRICAN AFFAIRS: Journal of the Royal African Society

Editors: Alison Smith and Anthony Atmore

Editorial address:
Royal African Society
18 Northumberland Avenue
London WC2N 5BJ, England

Sponsor: same as above

Frequency: Q
Subscription: $9/£3.50

Founded: 1901
Subscribers: 2,300

Editorial interest:
Chronological: 1900 to present, current events
Geographical: Africa
Topical: anthropology, auxiliary historical disciplines, bibliographical articles, cultural affairs, demography, economics, education, foreign relations, geography, historiography, history of ideas, international organizations, legal and constitutional affairs, politics and government, social history, sociology

Editorial policies:
Query letter prior to submission of ms. optional
Style manual: Clarendon Press; a style sheet for contributors is available on request
Preferred length of ms.: 6,000-7,000 words; rarely and unwillingly accepts longer articles for serialization
Author payment: none, except in the case of specially commissioned articles; two journal copies and 25 article reprints
End notes. Accepts English- and French-language mss. Publishes articles in English, but French not entirely ruled out. Address mss. to the editors at the editorial address or to Alison Smith, Institute of Commonwealth Studies, Oxford University, Oxford, or Anthony Atmore, Centre for International and Area Studies, London University, London W.C.1. Potential authors should write for a university-level audience interested in interdisciplinary social sciences and for senior government service officers and comparable business executives. Wants mss. that concentrate on a specific area, which, while conforming to a high standard within a particular discipline, must

be intelligible to a general reader. In addition to the general topical focus of the journal listed above, the editors will consider mss. on agriculture, business, church or ecclesiastical, literature (history and criticism), and religious studies in exceptional cases. Moreover, the editors do not totally exclude mss. dealing with periods prior to 1900.

Notes: Articles abstracted in *African Abstracts*, HA

Special features: list of articles on African social science topics published in reputable journals not devoted to Africa. Potential contributors should submit the original and one copy of the ms., typed, double-spaced on quarto size paper along with a brief biographical note. Book reviews are assigned and solicited; rarely accepts freelance offerings; no remuneration.

AFRICAN ARTS

Editors: Paul O. Proehl and John F. Povey

Editorial address:
African Studies Center
University of California
Los Angeles, California 90024

Sponsor: same as above

Frequency: Q   Founded: 1967
Subscription: $12   Subscribers: 4,000

Editorial interest:
Chronological: unrestricted
Geographical: Africa
Topical: archaeology, art, cinema and film, cultural affairs, ethnology, folklore, literature (history and criticism), music (history), theatre and drama
Special scope: African poetry, fiction, painting, sculpture

Editorial policies:
Query prior to submission of ms.
Style manual: none prescribed, consult previous issues
Preferred length of ms.: 5,000-7,000 words; longer articles accepted for serialization
Author payment: $25 to non-Africans, $50 to Africans, and two article reprints
End notes. Accepts mss. in all languages. Publishes articles in English. Address mss. to John Povey. Potential authors should write for an audience interested in African culture. Wants mss. on any of the arts of Africa, traditional or contemporary. Original art work—poetry, fiction, painting, or sculpture—accepted only from citizens of African nations.

AFRICAN ARTS (cont'd)

Notes: Articles indexed in *Art Index*

Special features: "New Acquisitions" section (photographs and identifying data of pieces newly acquired by museums), "Current and Continuing Exhibitions" (listing of current exhibitions of African art in non-profit museums and a listing of American museums having permanent collections of African art).

Illustrations: black and white large glossy prints are preferable to negatives; color 2 x 2-inch transparencies are the best, but good quality 35mm slides can be used; please do not send Kodacolor negatives, as it is difficult to reproduce from them; captions in the form of numbers on mounts of color slides, number black and white prints on the back and supply caption material on separate sheet, do not write on the backs of prints with pencil or ballpoint pen; submit as many photographs as possible, do not cut off the tops or bottoms of objects, avoid extraneous materials in back or foreground. Potential contributors should submit typed, double-spaced mss. Legal-size paper unacceptable.

End footnotes, keep to minimum and integrate into the text where possible. Book reviews are assigned or solicited, but freelance offerings would be considered; no remuneration. Those interested in reviewing should write to book editor. Reports on submissions in one to two months.

AFRICAN CHALLENGE

Editor-in-chief: J. K. Bolarin

Editor: T. O. Onajobi

Editorial address:
Niger Challenge Publications
P.M.B. 12067
Lagos, Nigeria, West Africa

Sponsor: Sudan Interior Mission

Frequency: 10 xy
Subscription: 8s.6p. N£

Founded: 1951
Circulation: 35,000

Editorial interest:
Chronological: unrestricted (emphasis on current events)
Geographical: worldwide (especially Africa)
Topical: agriculture, bibliographical articles, church or ecclesiastical affairs, communications media, cultural affairs, education, geography, historiography, religious studies, transportation

Editorial policies:
Query prior to submission of ms. *Challenge* edits authors' mss. according to their own style manual.
Preferred length of ms.: approximately 1,000 words; longer articles accepted for serialization

AFRICAN CHALLENGE (cont'd)

Author payment: two guineas or more, depending on nature of ms., and three to five copies of article

End notes. Potential authors should write for an audience of students from primary and secondary schools mainly. Would like to see educational and entertaining articles, news features, and religious knowledge.

Notes: Articles abstracted or indexed in CC, SSHI

Special features: cartoons, stories told in drawings or photographs with few words. Contributors should note that *Challenge* does not publish anything on politics, ecumenism, nor any controversial subject such as healing or speaking in tongues. Freelance book reviews are accepted if the book is a "Christian book"; no remuneration. Reports on submissions in three to four weeks.

AFRICAN COMMUNIST

Editorial address:
39 Goodge Street
London W. 1, England

Sponsor: South African Communist Party

Frequency: Q

Subscription: $2 individual, surface; $4 individual, airmail

Founded: 1959

Circulation: approximately 6,000

Editorial interest:
Chronological: 1900 to the present, current events
Geographical: Africa, Eastern Europe (if related to Africa), Middle East, United States (if related to Africa)
Topical: history of ideas, philosophy, politics and government, social history
Special scope: Marxist-Leninist analysis

Editorial policies:
Query prior to submission of ms.
Style manual: any
Preferred length of ms.: depends on subject matter; no serialization
Author payment: cash in rare instances, and up to six copies of issue in which article appears
Bottom or end notes. Accepts mss. in any language, but prefers English. Publishes articles in English. Potential authors should write for an international African audience. Wants mss. dealing with Marxist-Leninist thought relating to African history and politics.

Notes: Book reviews are assigned and solicited; no remuneration. Persons interested in reviewing should write the editorial address. Editorial reports on submission within two weeks.

AFRICAN DEVELOPMENT

Editor: Alan Rake

Editorial address:
> John Carpenter House
> John Carpenter Street
> London EC4Y 0AX, England

Frequency: M

Founded: 1966

Subscription: £5.50, surface; £6.75, airmail

Subscribers: 4,650

Editorial interest:
> Chronological: current events
> Geographical: Africa
> Topical: agriculture, business, communications media, economics, foreign relations, international organizations, politics and government, science and technology, transportation
> Special scope: development

Editorial policies:
> Query prior to submission of ms.
> Style manual: unspecified
> Preferred length of ms.: short items, 50 words; full length articles, 800-1,600 words; rarely accepts longer articles for serialization
> Author payment: £15 per 1,000 words, and one copy of issue in which article appears
> No reference notes. Accepts mss. in English or French on arrangement. Articles published in English. Potential authors should write for an audience of businessmen, economists, and civil servants.

Notes:
> Special feature: analysis of current African economic problems. Freelance book reviews are considered; some remuneration. Editorial reports on submissions within one month.

AFRICAN LANGUAGE STUDIES

Editor: W. H. Whiteley

Editorial address:
> School of Oriental and African Studies
> University of London
> London W.C. 1, England

Sponsor: same as above

Frequency: A

Founded: 1960

Subscription: £3

Editorial interest:
> Chronological: unrestricted
> Geographical: Africa
> Topical: language (philology, semantics), literature (history and criticism)

AFRICAN LANGUAGE STUDIES (cont'd)

Editorial policies:
> Query prior to submission of ms.
> Style manual: "Notes to Contributors of ALS" available on request
> Preferred length of ms.: 2,000-10,000 words; no serialization
> Author payment: 20 article reprints
> End notes. Contributors are normally past or present members or students of the school. Accepts mss. and publishes articles in English or French. Potential authors should write for professionals in African languages and literature.

Notes: Articles abstracted in *African Abstracts*. No book reviews. Editorial reports on submissions in four to six weeks.

AFRICAN LAW DIGEST

Editor: Sarah Sapir Eisen

Editorial address:
> Box 58
> 435 West 116th Street
> New York, New York 10027

Sponsor: African Law Center, Columbia University

Frequency: Q

Subscription: varies for individuals and organizations

Founded: 1966

Subscribers: approximately 300

Editorial interest:
> Chronological: current events
> Geographical: Africa
> Topical: legal and constitutional affairs

Editorial policies:
> A staff-written digest of contemporary African law developments.

AFRICAN LAW STUDIES

Editor: Sarah Sapir Eisen

Editorial address:
> Box 58
> 435 West 116th Street
> New York, New York 10027

Sponsor: African Law Center, Columbia University

Frequency: BM

Subscription: $5

Founded: 1969

Subscribers: approximately 300

AFRICAN LAW STUDIES (cont'd)

Editorial interest:
    Chronological: current events
    Geographical: Africa
    Topical: legal and constitutional affairs

Editorial policies:
    Style manual: any
    Preferred length of ms.: 25 typed pages; occasionally accepts longer
        articles for serialization
    Author payment: 25 article reprints
    End notes. Accepts mss. and publishes articles in English. Potential
        authors should write for an audience of lawyers, law teachers, and
        law students. Wants legal surveys, selective bibliographies of areas
        of African law, and analysis of legal systems in order to provide a
        tool for research and information concerning current developments
        in African law that are not adequately presented elsewhere.

Notes: Articles indexed in ILP. No book reviews.

AFRICAN LITERATURE TODAY

Editor: Eldred D. Jones

Editorial address:
    Department of English
    Fourah Bay College
    University of Sierra Leone
    Mount Aureol
    Freetown, Sierra Leone

Frequency: A   Founded: 1968
Subscription: $8

Editorial interest:
    Chronological: unrestricted
    Geographical: Africa
    Topical: literature (history and criticism)

Editorial policies:
    Query prior to submission of ms.
    Style manual: MLA Style Sheet
    Preferred length of ms.: 1,000-3,000 words; no serialization
    Author payment: 1 copy of issue in which article appears, and article
        reprints at cost
    End notes. Accepts mss. and publishes articles in English. Potential
        authors should write for an audience of university teachers and
        students as well as school teachers and high school seniors. Wants
        mss. on African literature that focus on explanatory criticism rather
        than those of a polemical nature. Authors are advised to focus on a
        single topic (e.g., individual works or groups of works) rather than
        generalities.

AFRICAN LITERATURE TODAY (cont'd)

Notes: Articles indexed in SSHI
> Special feature: cumulative bibliography. Book reviews are assigned or solicited, but freelance offerings are considered if they fit into the genre of the current number in preparation; some remuneration. "Since *African Literature Today* is published annually with a focus on a particular genre a potential author who has fortunately written on the decided topic will receive word about his ms. within a month, otherwise he will be notified immediately how long he will have to await an editorial decision."

AFRICAN MUSIC: Journal of the African Music Society

Editors: Hugh Tracey and Andrew Tracey

Editorial address:
P.O. Box 138
Roodepoort, Transvaal, South Africa

Sponsor: African Music Society

Frequency: A

Subscription: Rds 4 in South Africa; $5.75 elsewhere

Founded: 1954

Subscribers: approximately 500

Editorial interest:
> Chronological: unrestricted, including the future of African music and its value to African society
> Geographical: Africa
> Topical: art, education, language (semantics), music (history), sociology, theatre and drama
> Special scope: dancing, discography, folk music, poetry, social anthropology, all relating to African music throughout the continent

Editorial policies:
> Query prior to submission of ms.
> Style manual: none prescribed
> Preferred length of ms.: about 2,000 words; accepts longer articles for serialization
> Author payment: 20 article reprints
> Bottom or end notes. Accepts mss. and publishes articles in English (mostly) or French. Potential authors should write for all persons, students, musicians interested in the whole subject of African indigenous music, instrumental or oral, and its relationship to African society. Wants mss. that are the result of original research work in the field on any aspect of African music and allied subjects, both technical and aesthetic. This includes semantics, poetry, stories, dancing, musical instruments, discs, etc.

Notes:
> Special feature: new techniques of music notation now being evolved for African musicians. Illustrations of ms. text should be clear in black

and white. Clear photographs acceptable, prints or negatives. Notations on illustrations or photos should be ready for the printer. Freelance book reviews are welcomed; no remuneration. Persons interested in reviewing should contact the editors. Editorial reports on submissions within a few days.

AFRICAN NOTES: Bulletin of the Institute of African Studies, University of Ibadan

Editor: Bolanle Awe

Editorial address:
> Institute of African Studies
> University of Ibadan
> Ibadan, Nigeria

Sponsor: same as above

Frequency: SA   Founded: 1963
Subscription: NL 1. ls.

Editorial interest:
> Chronological: unrestricted
> Geographical: Africa, Latin America, United States, West Indies
> Topical: agriculture, anthropology, archaeology, art, cultural affairs, demography, economics, ethnology, folklore, geography, historiography, language (philology, semantics), legal and constitutional affairs, literature (history and criticism), medicine (history), music (history), philosophy, politics and government, religious studies, research methods, social history, sociology, theatre and drama

Editorial policies:
> Style manual: none prescribed
> Preferred length of ms.: 10,000 words maximum; serialization acceptable
> Author payment: 20 article reprints
> Bottom or end notes. Accepts English-, French-, and Russian-language mss. Publishes articles in English. Potential authors should write for an academic audience with an interest in Africa. Wants mss. on African studies of an interdisciplinary nature that show new methods and techniques of obtaining evidence.

Notes: Abstracted in *African Abstracts*. Book reviews are assigned and solicited, but freelance offerings are also accepted; no remuneration. Persons interested in reviewing should contact the editor. Editorial reports on submissions in about one month.

AFRICAN PROGRESS

Editor: Linus A. Bassey

Editorial address:
114 E. 32nd Street
New York, New York 10016

Sponsor: Africa Investors and Placement Services Inc., New York, New York

Frequency: M
Subscription: $10

Founded: 1971
Subscribers: 10,000

Editorial interest:
Chronological: unrestricted
Geographical: Africa, Canada, United States
Topical: agriculture, art, business, communications media, cultural affairs, discovery and exploration, economics, education, ethnology, foreign relations, geography, international organization, language (philology and semantics), legal and constitutional affairs, medicine (history), military affairs, music (history), politics and government, science and technology, social history, transportation
Special scope: Black business enterprises

Editorial policies:
Query prior to submission of ms.
Style manual: available upon request
Preferred length of ms.: 5-10 typed pages; longer articles considered for serialization
Author payment: varies; includes copies of magazine
Notes must be in text. Accepts mss. in African languages, Arabic, English, or French: primarily English-language publication. Prefers articles dealing with African economic development, contemporary issues.

Notes: Articles cited in *Advertising Age*, "most African newspapers," *African World*, *Amsterdam News*, *Black News*, *Interlink*, *Jet Magazine*. Book reviews assigned. Editorial reports on submissions in two months.

AFRICAN QUARTERLY

Editor: D. Lincoln

Editorial address:
43 Great Russell Street
London, W.C. 1, England

Sponsor: Kegan Paul, Trench, Truber & Co.

Frequency: irr.
Subscription: gratis

Founded: 1963
Circulation: 2,750

Editorial interest:
Chronological: unrestricted
Geographical: Africa
Topical: unrestricted

AFRICAN QUARTERLY (cont'd)

Editorial policies:
> A dealer's catalog divided into (I) New Publications and (II) Second-hand Books. Authors of books and monographs on Africa are invited to alert the editor to the publication of their works.

Editors' note:
> Although this journal does not accept any mss., it is included because it contains extensive listings of works on Africa and therefore might aid scholars in their research.

AFRICAN RESEARCH AND DOCUMENTATION

Editor: Mrs. M. Johnson

Assistant editor: Mr. H. Hannam

Editorial address:
> Centre of West African Studies
> University of Birmingham
> P.O. Box 363
> Birmingham B13 9SA, England

Sponsor: African Studies Association of the United Kingdom (ASAUK) and the Standing Conference of Library Materials on Africa (SCOLMA)

Frequency: TA

Subscription: £2 with professional membership to ASAUK; £1, individual associate membership to ASAUK; £5, corporate associate membership to either ASAUK or SCOLMA

Founded: 1973; supersedes *Bulletin of the African Studies Association of the United Kingdom* and *Library Materials on Africa*

Editorial interest:
> Chronological: unrestricted
> Geographical: Africa
> Topical: unrestricted
> Special scope: research in progress in the United Kingdom, bibliographical articles and reviews

Editorial policies:
> Query prior to submission of ms.
> Style manual: none prescribed
> Preferred length of ms.: 750 words; no serialization
> Author payment: none
> Accepts mss. and publishes reports in English. Potential authors should write for university research workers. While United Kingdom research and events are of primary interest, information from other parts of the world, and particularly from Africa, will be welcomed.

Notes: Advance notice of conferences and seminars of interest to Africanists. A running record of research in progress in various fields of African studies in the United Kingdom. No book reviews.

AFRICAN REVIEW: A Journal of African Politics, Development and International Affairs

Editorial board: Nathan Shamuyarira, Okwudiba Nnoli, Irene Brown, and Anthony Rweyemamu

Editorial address:
Department of Political Science
University of Dar es Salaam
P.O. Box 35042
Dar es Salaam, Tanzania

Sponsor: same as above

Frequency: Q   Founded: 1971
Subscription: Tanzanian shillings 401
in Africa; $7.50 outside Africa

Editorial interest:
Chronological: unrestricted
Geographical: Africa
Topical: foreign relations, international organizations, politics, and government
Special scope: development

Editorial policies:
Query prior to submission of ms. optional
Style manual: none prescribed, consult previous issues
Preferred length of ms.: 4,000-5,000 words; no serialization
Author payment: 15 article reprints
End notes. Accepts English- and Swahili-language mss., publishes articles in English. Potential authors should write for an international audience of Africans, Europeans, and Americans. Wants mss. that reflect the realities of African politics, development, and international affairs. "The board of editors applies no rigid rules. No particular perspective is favored. Emphasis is on scope and depth of the African reality that is reflected in the ms."

Notes: Potential authors should submit two copies of the ms. Article and book review mss. should be accompanied by information on the author's professional status.

AFRICAN SCHOLAR: Journal of Research and Analysis, Quarterly Journal of the African Academy of Political and Social Sciences

Editor: J. B. C. Ugokwe

Editorial address:
P.O. Box 6555
Washington, D.C. 20009

Sponsor: African Academy of Political and Social Science, Inc.

Frequency: Q   Founded: 1969
Subscription: $5   Circulation: 5,000

AFRICAN SCHOLAR (cont'd)

Editorial interest:
> Chronological: unrestricted
> Geographical: Africa
> Topical: anthropology, auxiliary historical disciplines, cultural affairs, economics, education, ethnology, foreign relations, international organizations, language (philology, semantics), legal and constitutional affairs, philosophy, politics and government, religious studies, social history, sociology

Editorial policies:
> Style manual: any
> Preferred length of ms.: unrestricted
> Author payment: negotiable, and up to 10 article reprints
> Bottom or end notes. Accepts mss. and publishes articles in English. Wants analytical research mss. on political and social sciences.

Notes:
> Special feature: top regular columnists. Book reviews are assigned; no remuneration.

AFRICAN SOCIAL RESEARCH

Editors: J. Van Velson and Ian Henderson

Assistant editor: E. Haddon

Editorial address:
> Institute of African Studies
> University of Zambia
> P.O. Box 900
> Lusaka, Zambia

Sponsor: same as above

Frequency: SA

Subscription: $11.50 (includes one communication and one Zambian paper annually)

Founded: 1944 as *Rhodesia-Livingston Institute Journal: Human Problems in British Central Africa*

Subscribers: 408

Editorial interest:
> Chronological: unrestricted
> Geographical: Africa, Central Africa, Zambia
> Topical: unrestricted
> Special scope: human problems in Central Africa

Editorial policies:
> Query with 200-word summary prior to submission of ms.
> Style manual: "Notes for Contributors" available on request
> Preferred length of ms.: 5,000-10,000 words; no serialization
> Author payment: 25 article reprints

AFRICAN SOCIAL RESEARCH (cont'd)

End notes. Accepts mss. and publishes articles in English. Address mss.
to the publications officer at the editorial address. Potential authors
should write for an academic audience. Wants mss. on African
social research, especially social anthropology, psychology, economics, human geography, history and political science, with particular
reference to Zambia and Central African countries.

Notes: Abstracted or indexed in *Africa, African Abstracts, Current Geographical Publications*, HA, SSHI. Potential contributors should submit the
original and one copy of the ms., typed, double-spaced on quarto size
paper with generous margins. Book reviews are assigned; no remuneration. Persons interested in reviewing should contact the editors. Editorial
reports on submission within about two months after receipt of ms.

AFRICAN STUDIES

Editors: D. T. Cole and W. D. Hammond-Tooke

Editorial address:
Publications Officer
Witwatersrand University Press
Jan Smuts Avenue
Johannesburg, South Africa

Sponsor: same as above

Frequency: Q
Subscription: Rds 5.

Founded: 1921 (as *Bantu Studies*, title changed 1942)
Subscribers: approximately
600

Editorial interest:
Chronological: unrestricted
Geographical: Africa
Topical: anthropology, cultural affairs, education, folklore, language
(philology, semantics), politics and government

Editorial policies:
Style manual: style sheet available on request
Preferred length of ms.: about 25 typed pages; serialization acceptable
Author payment: 45 article reprints
End notes. Accepts Afrikaans- and English-language mss., and also mss.
in French or Portuguese if topic concerns territories in which these
languages are used. Will also accept African-language mss. if
accompanied by an Afrikaans, English, French, or Portuguese translation. Publishes articles in Afrikaans, English, French, or Portuguese.
Wants mss. of an academic and scholarly nature based on research of
a high academic standard and relevant to subject covered by journal.

Notes: Abstracted or indexed in APS, CC, HA. Potential authors are requested
to use special symbols only when really necessary. Book reviews are solicited; no remuneration.

42

AFRICAN STUDIES REVIEW

Editor: John P. Henderson

Editorial address:
   African Studies Center
   Michigan State University
   East Lansing, Michigan 48823

Sponsor: African Studies Association and the African Studies Center

Frequency: TA

Subscription: $18 members of the African
   Studies Association; $12 students;
   $25 institutional

Founded: 1962 (as *African Studies Bulletin*)

Subscribers: 2,140

Editorial interest:
   Chronological: unrestricted
   Geographical: Africa
   Topical: agriculture, anthropology, art, auxiliary historical disciplines,
      bibliographical articles, business, economics, education, folklore,
      foreign relations, geography, historiography, language (philology,
      semantics), literature (history and criticism), philosophy of history,
      politics and government, religious studies, science and technology,
      social history, sociology, theatre and drama

Editorial policies:
   Style manual: Chicago
   Preferred length of ms.: 20-25 typed pages; accepts longer articles for
      serialization
   Author payment: 10 article reprints
   Footnotes to be incorporated into the text. Accepts mss. and publishes
      articles in English or French. Address mss. to John P. Henderson,
      Department of Economics, Michigan State University, East
      Lansing, Michigan 48823. Potential authors should write for an
      audience of professional Africanists.

Notes:
   Special feature: "Brief Comments" on items of professional interest.
      Book reviews are assigned and solicited, but freelance offerings
      are considered; no remuneration. Reviews should be addressed to
      Kenneth C. Wylie, Book Review Editor, Herbert H. Lehman
      College, City University of New York, New York, N.Y.

AFRICAN URBAN NOTES

Editor: Ruth Simms Hamilton

Editorial address:
   African Studies Center
   Michigan State University
   East Lansing, Michigan 48823

Sponsor: same as above

AFRICAN URBAN NOTES (cont'd)

Frequency: Q

Subscription: free only to scholars and institutions engaged in urban African research, may move to subscription

Founded: 1966

Circulation: approximately 500

Editorial interest:
    Chronological: unrestricted
    Geographical: Africa
    Topical: anthropology, architecture, auxiliary historical disciplines, bibliographical articles, business, communications media, cultural affairs, demography, historiography, history of ideas, international organizations, legal and constitutional affairs, maritime history, medicine (history), military affairs, politics and government, research methods, science and technology, social history, sociology, transportation
    Special scope: urbanology

Editorial policies:
    Query letter prior to submission of ms., since all mss. are solicited by guest editors
    Style manual: Chicago or *American Anthropologist*
    Preferred length of ms.: 15-30 typed pages; no serialization to date
    Author payment: four article reprints
    Bibliographical reference notes at end of ms., explanatory notes at bottom of page. Solicits mss. and publishes articles in English.

Notes:
    Special feature: research reports, proposed projects; bibliographical supplements on specific topics are also issued. No book reviews.

AFRICANA BULLETIN

Editor: Bogadar Winid

Editorial address:
    Centre of African Studies
    University of Warsaw
    Warszawa 63,
    Krakowskie Przedmieście 26/28, Poland

Sponsor: same as above

Frequency: SA

Subscription: $7

Founded: 1964

Subscribers: 300

Editorial interest:
    Chronological: unrestricted
    Geographical: Africa
    Topical: unrestricted

AFRICANA BULLETIN (cont'd)

Editorial policies:
>Query prior to submission of ms.
>
>Style manual: Oxford University Press
>
>Preferred length of ms.: 20-30 typed pages; no serialization
>
>Author payment: 25 article reprints
>
>End notes. Article-length mss. accepted from Polish Africanists only. Accepts English-, French-, and Polish-language mss. Publishes articles in English or French. Wants mss. on contemporary African problems.

Notes:
>Special feature: Polish "Africana." Book reviews are assigned, but free-lance offerings are considered. Persons interested in book reviewing should contact the editor. Editorial reports on submissions in six months.

AFRICANA LIBRARY JOURNAL: A Quarterly Bibliography and News Bulletin

Editor: John Webster

Editorial address:
>Africana Publishing Corp.
>
>101 Fifth Avenue
>
>New York, New York 10003

Frequency: Q   Founded: 1970

Subscription: $15 individual; $25 institutional Subscribers: 377

Editorial interest:
>Chronological: unrestricted
>
>Geographical: Africa
>
>Topical: bibliographical articles

Editorial policies:
>Query prior to submission of ms.
>
>Style manual: none prescribed, consult previous issues
>
>Preferred length of ms.: none
>
>Author payment: two copies of issue in which article appears; off-prints can be arranged
>
>End notes. Accepts English-, French-, German-, Italian-, Portuguese-, Russian-, Spanish-, and Swahili-language mss.

Notes: A bibliographical publication
>Special features: bibliography, checklist, acquisitions guide, news and notes, audiovisual information, bio-bibliographies. Those interested in book reviewing should write the editor. Editorial decisions on submissions as soon as possible, no set time.

AFRICANA MARBURGENSIA

Editors: Herrmann Jungraithmayr and Hans-Jürgen Greschat

Editorial address:
Krummbogen 28
355 Marburg-Lahn, Federal Republic of Germany

Frequency: TA   Founded: 1968
Subscription: unreported   Subscribers: 400

Editorial interest:
Chronological: unrestricted
Geographical: Africa
Topical: anthropology, church or ecclesiastical affairs, discovery and
exploration, geography, historiography, language (philology,
semantics), legal and constitutional affairs, music (history),
religious studies, research methods

Editorial policies:
Style manual: none prescribed
Preferred length of ms.: 5-8 typed pages
Author payment: 10 article reprints
Bottom notes. Accepts mss. and publishes articles in English, French, or
German

Notes: No book reviews. Editorial decision on submissions in one month.

AFRICANA NEWS AND NOTES

Director: Miss A. H. Smith

Editorial address:
Africana Museum
Public Library
Markel Square
Johannesburg, South Africa

Sponsor: same as above

Frequency: Q   Founded: 1943
Subscription: Rds 2.   Subscribers: 489

Editorial interest:
Chronological: unrestricted
Geographical: Africa (south of the Zambesi River)
Topical: unrestricted (excepting politics)
Special scope: items of interest to collectors of Africana, numismatics

Editorial policies:
Query prior to submission of ms.
Style manual: none prescribed
Preferred length of ms.: 5,000 words maximum; longer articles for
serialization rarely accepted
Author payment: 10 copies of issue in which article appears
End notes. Accepts mss. and publishes articles in Afrikaans, Dutch, or

AFRICANA NEWS AND NOTES (cont'd)

English. Address mss. to the director. Potential authors should write for an audience of collectors of Africana. Wants mss. covering books, maps, pictures, numismatics, furniture, and other objects relating to Africa south of the Zambesi River. Illustrations are welcomed.

Notes: Abstracted or indexed in HA, *Index to South African Periodicals*
Special features: collectors' notes on unusual items related to South Africa (such as cigarette cards, match box labels, medals, pictures, etc.). Book reviews are staff-written.

AFRICANA RESEARCH BULLETIN

Editors: J. G. Edowu Hyde and James A. S. Blair

Editorial address:
Institute of African Studies
Fourah Bay College
Freetown, Sierra Leone

Sponsor: same as above

Frequency: Q   Founded: 1970
Subscription: $3   Subscribers: 150

Editorial interest:
Chronological: unrestricted
Geographical: Africa, Sierra Leone (mainly)
Topical: anthropology, archaeology, art, bibliographical articles, church or ecclesiastical affairs, cultural affairs, economics, ethnology, folklore, geography, language (philology, semantics), legal and constitutional affairs, literature (history and criticism), music (history), politics and government, social history, sociology, transportation

Editorial policies:
Query not necessary, provided manuscript is related to Sierra Leone
Preferred length of ms.: 10-25 typed pages; longer articles accepted for serialization
Author payment: 20 complimentary reprints of article
End notes. Editors would like to see contributions from "all those many visiting scholars who have had the privilege to work and do research in Sierra Leone and who have carried their achievements with them to where they are inaccessible for Sierra Leoneans."

Notes:
Special feature: bibliographic listings of Sierra Leoneana. Contributors should note that at present photographs and drawings will not be reproduced. Freelance book reviews are accepted; no remuneration. Reports on submissions in two weeks to one month.

AFRIKA SPECTRUM

Editor: Lothar Voss

Editorial address:
Deutsches Institut für Afrika-Forschung
Kloster Wall 4
2 Hamburg 1
Federal Republic of Germany

Sponsor: same as above

Frequency: TA   Founded: 1966
Subscription: DM36   Subscribers: 262

Editorial interest:
Chronological: 1900 to present
Geographical: Africa
Topical: agriculture, anthropology, bibliographical articles, church or
ecclesiastical affairs, communications media, discovery and exploration, economics, foreign relations, frontier areas, geography,
historiography, international organizations, legal and constitutional affairs, military affairs, politics and government, research
methods, sociology, transportation

Editorial policies:
Query prior to submission of ms.
Style manual: none prescribed
Preferred length of ms.: approximately 5,000 words; no serialization
Author payment: approximately DM250 and 30 article reprints
Bottom or end notes. Accepts mss. and publishes articles in English,
French, or German. Potential authors should address themselves to
scientists and research workers. Seeks mss. dealing with research
methods.

Notes: Articles abstracted or indexed in CARDAN: *Bulletin d'Information et
de Liaison* [Paris], CIDESA: *Bulletin of Information on Current
Research on Human Societies Concerning Africa*, SSHI.
Special features: survey of Africa legislation from 50 African government
gazettes and regional organizations. The Institute also welcomes
shorter mss. describing the research and programs of non-German
institutes of African affairs; remuneration approximately DM100.
Book reviews are assigned; pays DM25 per review. Reports on
submissions within one to two weeks.

AFRO-AMERICAN STUDIES: An Interdisciplinary Journal

Editor: Richard D. Trent

Editorial address:
1127 Carroll Street
Brooklyn, New York 11225

Sponsor: Gordon & Breach Science Publishers, Inc.

AFRO-AMERICAN STUDIES (cont'd)

Frequency: Q   Founded: 1970
Subscription: $11

Editorial interest:
> Chronological: unrestricted
> Geographical: Africa, Latin America, United States, West Indies
> Topical: anthropology, art, business, communications media, cultural
> affairs, economics, education, ethnology, folklore, foreign rela-
> tions, history of ideas, international organizations, language
> (philology, semantics), legal and constitutional affairs, literature
> (history and criticism), medicine (history), politics and govern-
> ment, religious studies, science and technology, social history,
> sociology

Editorial policies:
> Style manual: Chicago or Oxford University Press
> Preferred length of ms.: 15-25 typed pages; longer articles for serializa-
> tion considered
> Author payment: 50 article reprints
> Bottom or end notes. Accepts mss. and publishes articles in English.
> Wants "relevant, meaningful, well-organized, interesting, readable
> mss. on the Afro-American."

Notes:
> Special features: documents and announcements. Potential authors
> should use a uniform style, submit a two- to three-sentence
> abstract, the original and one copy of the ms. Book reviews are
> assigned and solicited, but freelance offerings are considered; no
> remuneration.

AGRICULTURAL ECONOMICS BULLETIN FOR AFRICA

Editor: St. George C. Cooper

Editorial address:
> Economic Commission for Africa
> Box 3001
> Addis Ababa, Ethiopia

Sponsor: United Nations

Frequency: SA   Founded: 1962
Subscription: not reported

Editorial interest:
> Chronological: current events
> Geographical: Africa
> Topical: agriculture, economics

Editorial policies:
> Style manual: "Notes on Contributions" printed on cover of journal
> Preferred length of ms.: 15-30 typed pages

AGRICULTURAL ECONOMICS BULLETIN FOR AFRICA (cont'd)

Author payment: 20 article reprints
Bottom notes. Accepts mss. and publishes articles in English or French.
Wants mss. on agricultural and economic development.

Notes: Editorial reports on submissions in one month.

AMERICAN PORTUGUESE CULTURAL SOCIETY JOURNAL

Editor: Frank M. Folsom

Editorial address:
29 Broadway
New York, New York 10005

Sponsor: American Portuguese Cultural Society

Frequency: Q   Founded: 1966
Subscription: unreported   Subscribers: 891

Editorial interest:
Chronological: unrestricted
Geographical: Africa, Asia, Brazil, Middle East, Western Europe
(Portuguese territories, past and present)
Topical: unrestricted (exception: no political writings)

Editorial policies:
Query prior to submission of ms.
Style manual: Chicago
Preferred length of ms.: 1,500-3,000 words; serialization acceptable
Author payment: $50 to correspondents for mailing and typing expenses,
12 article reprints
End notes

Notes:
Special features: suggested topics for research. Book reviews are
assigned and solicited; same remuneration as for articles. Editorial
decision on submissions within two weeks.

ANNUAL REPORT OF THE SOUTH AFRICAN INSTITUTE OF RACE RELATIONS

Editor: R. M. de Villiers

Editorial address:
South African Institute of Race Relations
P.O. Box 97
Johannesburg, South Africa

Sponsor: same as above

Frequency: A   Founded: 1929
Subscription: gratis   Circulation: 5,500

ANNUAL REPORT OF THE SOUTH AFRICAN INSTITUTE OF RACE RELATIONS (cont'd)

Editorial interest:
> Chronological: current events
> Geographical: South Africa
> Special scope: race relations

Editorial policies:
> Staff written. Annual report of the Institute's activities.

ANTIQUARIES JOURNAL: Journal of the Society of Antiquaries of London

Assistant secretary: F. H. Thompson

Editorial address:
> Society of Antiquaries
> Burlington House, Piccadilly
> London W1V 0HS, England

Sponsor: same as above

Frequency: SA
Subscription: £7/$18

Founded: 1921
Subscribers: approximately 500

Editorial interest:
> Chronological: pre-history to 1800
> Geographical: Africa, Middle East, Western Europe
> Topical: archaeology, architecture, art

Editorial policies:
> Query prior to submission of ms. optional
> Style manual: Oxford University Press
> Preferred length of ms.: 2,000-15,000 words; accepts longer or continuing annual reports on excavations for serialization
> Author payment: 25 article reprints or six reprints of short "Notes"
> Accepts mss. and publishes articles in English. Potential authors should write for Fellows of the Society, which includes archaeologists, antiquarians, and historians.

Notes: Articles cited in *British Humanities Index*.
> Special features: acquisitions by the Society's Library, abstracts of British and foreign periodical literature. Contributors should submit line or photographic illustrations suitable for reduction. Book reviews are solicited; small remuneration, since books are returned to the Society's Library.

ARCHAEOLOGIA: Miscellaneous Tracts Relating to Antiquity

Assistant secretary: F. H. Thompson

Editorial address:
Society of Antiquaries
Burlington House, Piccadilly
London W1V 0HS, England

Sponsor: same as above

Frequency: once every 18 months to
2 years
Subscription: £5

Founded: 1770
Subscribers: approximately
250

Editorial interest:
Chronological: pre-history to 1800
Geographical: Africa, Middle East, Western Europe
Topical: archaeology, architecture, art

Editorial policies:
Query prior to submission of ms. optional
Style manual: Oxford University Press
Preferred length of ms.: 5,000-30,000 words
Author payment: 25 article reprints
Bottom or end notes. Accepts mss. and publishes articles in English.
Potential contributors should write for Fellows of the Society,
which includes archaeologists, antiquarians, and historians.
Wants mss. of high professional standard.

Notes: All illustrations (line or photo) accompanying mss. must be suitable
for reduction.

ARCHIV ORIENTALNI

Editor-in-chief: L. Matous

Editorial address:
Oriental Institute of the Czechoslovak Academy of Sciences
Lázenská 4
Prague 4, Czechoslovakia

Sponsor: same as above

Frequency: Q
Subscription: $15

Founded: 1932
Subscribers: approximately
1,000

Editorial interest:
Chronological: unrestricted
Geographical: Africa, Asia, Eastern Europe, Middle East, Pacific Area,
USSR (Central Asia)
Topical: anthropology, archaeology, architecture, art, auxiliary histori-
cal disciplines, bibliographical articles, communications media,
cultural affairs, demography, discovery and exploration, economics,

ARCHIV ORIENTALNI (cont'd)

education, ethnology, folklore, foreign relations, historiography, history of ideas, international law, international organization, language (philology, semantics), legal and constitutional affairs, literature (history and criticism), maritime history, medicine (history), military affairs, music (history), naval affairs, philosophy, philosophy of history, politics and government, religious studies, research methods, social history, sociology, theatre and drama, transportation

Editorial policies:

Query prior to submission of ms.

Style manual: any

Preferred length of ms.: 20 typed pages maximum; longer articles for serialization accepted in exceptional cases

Author payment: 65 article reprints

Bottom or end notes. Accepts mss. and publishes articles in English, French, German, or Russian. Potential authors should write for a scholarly audience. Wants mss. on all subjects of Oriental studies.

Notes: Articles abstracted or cited in HA, *Orientalistische Literatur-Zeitung.* Book reviews are assigned; no remuneration. Persons interested in reviewing should contact the editor. Editorial reports on submissions in three to six months.

ASC NEWSLETTER

Editor: Marjorie K. Winters

Editorial address:
African Studies Center
Michigan State University
East Lansing, Michigan 48823

Sponsor: same as above

Frequency: BM   Founded: 1970
Subscription: gratis   Circulation: approximately
                                                  900

Editorial interest:
Chronological: unrestricted
Geographical: Africa
Topical: unrestricted
Special scope: current news and research notes

Editorial policies:
A staff-written newsletter. Published in English.

Notes:
Special features: information on grants-in-aid, scholarships, etc.; information on summer and regular programs on African studies centers throughout the world; listing of teaching aids, new methods,

new publications. No book reviews. The African Studies Center also publishes a monograph series.

ASIA AND AFRICA REVIEW (incorporating The Indian at Home and Overseas)

Editor: Dr. K. D. Kumria

Assistant editor: Anand Kumria

Editorial address:
38 Kennington Lane
London SE11 4LS, England

Frequency: M
Subscription: $4.50/£1.50

Founded: 1961
Subscribers: 1,500

Editorial interest:
Chronological: current events
Geographical: Africa, Asia, Middle East, West Indies
Topical: art, cultural affairs, economics, politics and government,
theatre and drama

Editorial policies:
Query prior to submission of ms.
Style manual: none prescribed, consult previous issues
Preferred length of ms.: 425-850 words
Author payment: cash by arrangement
Notes not normally used. Accepts mss. and publishes articles in English.
Wants mss. dealing with the current political, cultural, and economic
affairs of African and Asian peoples everywhere. Prefers themes
that support the policies of established regimes.

ASIAN AND AFRICAN STUDIES

Editor: Ivan Doležal

Executive editor: Jozef Genzor

Editorial address:
Department of Oriental Studies of the Slovak Academy of Sciences
Klememsova 27
Bratislava, Czechoslovakia

Sponsor: same as above

Frequency: A
Subscription: Kčs 30

Founded: 1965

Editorial interest:
Chronological: 1600 to present, current events
Geographical: Africa, Asia, Middle East, Pacific Area

Topical: anthropology, archaeology, art, cultural affairs, demography, education, ethnology, folklore, geography, historiography, history of ideas, language (philology, semantics), literature (history and criticism), politics and government, religious studies, social history, sociology, theatre and drama

Editorial policies:
Query prior to submission of ms.
Style manual: contact editor
Preferred length of ms.: 35 typed pages or less; longer articles for serialization subject to special consideration
Author payment: cash payable in Czech crowns only, and 10 article reprints
End notes. Publications by contributors who are not members of the Slovak Academy are limited to one article per annual. Accepts mss. and publishes articles in English, French, or German. Address ms. to the editor. Potential authors should write for a scholarly audience. Wants mss. on language, literature, or history of the Asian and African peoples.

Notes: Articles cited in *The Middle East and North Africa* (annual). Freelance book review offerings are welcomed and preferred. Editorial reports on submissions in about two months.

ASSEGAI: Magazine of the Rhodesian Army

Managing editor: Major E. G. Thomas

Assistant editor: I. M. Zimet

Editorial address:
Army Headquarters
P. B. 7720
Causeway, Rhodesia

Sponsor: Rhodesian Army

Frequency: M Founded: 1961
Subscription: R$1.50 Subscribers: 1,000

Editorial interest:
Chronological: nineteenth century to present; current events
Geographical: worldwide
Topical: air forces, communications media, discovery and exploration, folklore, foreign relations, frontier areas, international organizations, literature (history and criticism), military affairs, naval affairs

Editorial policies:
Style manual: literary style sheet
Preferred length of ms.: unrestricted; longer articles accepted for serialization

ASSEGAI (cont'd)

Author payment: complimentary article reprints as requested
Bottom or end notes. Would like to see articles of military interest, and concerning current affairs.

Notes: Book reviews accepted; query editor; no remuneration. Reports on submissions in one month.

AZANIA

Editor: Neville Chittick

Editorial address:
Box 7680
Nairobi, Kenya

Sponsor: British Institute of History and Archaeology in East Africa

Frequency: A
Subscription: free to members of the
Institute; $6 initiation fee

Founded: 1966
Subscribers: approximately
130

Editorial interest:
Chronological: c.1000 B.C. to the nineteenth century
Geographical: Africa
Topical: anthropology, archaeology
Special scope: Iron Age of Africa, Muslim towns on the East African coast, and pre-colonial East African history

Editorial policies:
Query prior to submission of ms.
Style manual: none prescribed, consult previous issues
Preferred length of ms.: 10,000 words; no serialization
Author payment: 25 article reprints, 10 reprints of "Notes" (one- to two-page articles)
End notes. Accepts mss. and publishes articles in English or French. Articles should be directed to an audience at the university research level. Seeks mss. based on original research and field reports from historians, anthropologists, and archaeologists working in Eastern Africa.

Notes: Abstracted in *African Abstracts*. Book reviews are assigned and solicited. Persons interested in reviewing should write the editor; 10 off-prints of review as remuneration. Editorial decisions on submissions normally within one month.

BA SHIRU

Editors: Syl Cheyney-Coker, Harold Scheub, and Laura Tanna

Editorial address:
Department of African Languages and Literature
University of Wisconsin
Madison, Wisconsin 53706

BA SHIRU (cont'd)

Frequency: SA	Founded: 1970
Subscription: $3	Subscribers: 500

Editorial interest:
> Chronological: unrestricted
> Geographical: Africa
> Topical: anthropology, art, auxiliary historical disciplines, communications media, education, folklore, foreign relations, language (philology, semantics), literature (history and criticism), music (history), politics and government, theatre and drama

Editorial policies:
> Style manual: style sheet available on request
> Preferred length of ms.: 500 words; serialization considered
> Author payment: varies according to contribution, and two article reprints
> End notes. Accepts English- and French-language mss., publishes in English. Contributors should present the African point of view. Desire mss. offering criticisms and major events related to Africa; political commentaries and discussions about Africa; essays on art, foreign affairs, and music; and poems, short stories, and one-act plays. "Mss. must be original and not too ambiguous, authorities honored or acknowledged to avoid plagiarizing. Our policy is to give students a wide range of topics on Africa and hopefully to reach a stream of consciousness with some of these features."

Notes: Cited in SSHI. Freelance book reviews welcomed. Persons interested in reviewing should write the editors; remuneration. Editorial decision on submissions within one month.

BEAU-COCOA

Editor: Lloyd Addison

Editorial address:
> P.O. Box 409
> New York, New York 10035

Frequency: SA	Founded: 1968
Subscription: $3	Subscribers: 200

Editorial interest:
> Chronological: unrestricted
> Geographical: worldwide
> Topical: architecture, art, church or ecclesiastical affairs, cinema and film, communications media, cultural affairs, discovery and exploration, economics, education, ethnology, folklore, foreign relations, history of ideas, language (philology, semantics), literature (history and criticism), philosophy, philosophy of history, sociology, theatre and drama

BEAU-COCOA (cont'd)

Special scope: aesthetics, poetry; historical matters are of little interest; emphasis is on creative composition

Editorial policies:

Query prior to submission of ms.

Preferred length of ms.: depending on quality and sustained interest, up to 1,500 words; no serialization

Author payment: approximately three issue copies; for major works can send approximately 20

Prefers references to be incorporated into ms. Potential authors should write for an essentially Black audience. Would like to see articles on new ideas, Black ethos, human destiny, and community action management.

Notes: Articles abstracted or indexed in *Writer's Market*, *Black List*

Special features: stylistic trends in creative composition. All mss. must be retyped for offset. Book reviews are not solicited; potential reviewers should try to review pertinent material. Reports on submissions in approximately two weeks.

BLACK ACADEMY REVIEW: A Quarterly of the Black World

Editor: S. Okechukwu Mezu

Editorial address:

Black Academy Press, Inc.
135 University Avenue
Buffalo, New York 14214

Frequency: Q

Founded: 1970

Subscription: $7 individual, $4 student

Subscribers: 5,000

Editorial interest:

Chronological: unrestricted (mainly twentieth century)

Geographical: Africa, Canada, Latin America, United States, West Indies

Topical: anthropology, archaeology, architecture, art, auxiliary historical disciplines, bibliographical articles, cultural affairs, education, ethnology, folklore, historiography, history of ideas, international organizations, language (philology, semantics), literature (history and criticism), music (history), philosophy, religious studies, social history, sociology, theatre and drama

Special scope: Black civilization

Editorial policies:

Style manual: consult previous issues

Preferred length of ms.: 2,000-10,000 words; occasionally accepts longer articles for serialization

Author payment: monetary and article reprint remuneration varies

End notes. Accepts mss. in English and exceptionally in French. Articles published in English. Potential authors should write for a college and academic audience.

BLACK ACADEMY REVIEW (cont'd)

Notes:
> Special features: bibliographical review essays, reports on conferences.
> Freelance book reviews are considered.

BLACK ARTS MAGAZINE

Editors: David Rambeau and Demon Smith

Editorial address:
> 401 East Adams
> Detroit, Michigan 48226

Sponsor: Project BAIT (Black Awareness In Television)

Frequency: SA   Founded: 1964
Subscription: $3   Subscribers: 100

Editorial interest:
> Chronological: current events
> Geographical: Africa, Latin America, United States, West Indies
> Topical: art (cartoons), cinema and film, communications media,
> > cultural affairs, education, literature (poetry), theatre and drama
>
> Special scope: Pan-Africanism

Editorial policies:
> Query prior to submission of ms.
> Preferred length of ms.: 1-10 typed pages; no serialization
> Author payment: 10 copies of issue
> Bottom notes. Would like to see articles on drama, electronic communi-
> > cations, and film. Articles should demonstrate serious involvement
> > with the subject.

Notes: Freelance book reviews accepted; no remuneration. Reports on submissions in two to three weeks.

BLACK CREATION: A Quarterly Review of Black Arts and Letters

Editor: Fred Beauford

Editorial address:
> 10 Washington Place, Fifth Floor
> New York, New York 10003

Sponsor: Institute of Afro-American Affairs

Frequency: Q   Founded: 1970
Subscription: $4   Subscribers: 900

Editorial interest:
> Chronological: unrestricted
> Geographical: Africa, Canada, Pacific Area, United States, West Indies
> Topical: art, cinema and film, cultural affairs, literature (history and
> > criticism), music (history), theatre and drama

BLACK CREATION (cont'd)

Editorial policies:
> Query prior to submission of ms.
> Style manual: none prescribed
> Preferred length of ms.: 8-20 typed pages; no serialization
> Author payment: article reprints as requested
> Accepts mss. and publishes articles in English. Articles should be
>> written for an audience interested in the arts.

Notes: Freelance book reviews are considered; those interested in reviewing
should write the book review editor, Jim Walker. Reports on submissions
in two months.

BLACK ENTERPRISE: For Black Men and Women Who Want to Get Ahead

Editor: Earl G. Graves

Managing editor: Robert J. Imbriano

Editorial address:
> 295 Madison Avenue
> New York, New York 10017

Frequency: M   Founded: 1969
Subscription: $10 in U.S., $12 elsewhere

Editorial interest:
> Chronological: current events
> Geographical: Africa, Canada, United States, West Indies
> Topical: business, economics, foreign relations, politics and
>> government

Editorial policies:
> Query prior to submission of ms.
> Style manual: consult previous issues
> Preferred length of ms.: 2,000-5,000 words
> Author payment: none
> No notes.

BLACK SCHOLAR: Journal of Black Studies and Research

Editor: Robert Chrisman

Managing editor: Robert Allen

Editorial address:
> Box 908
> Sausalito, California 94965

Sponsor: Black World Foundation

Frequency: 10 xy   Founded: 1969
Subscription: $10, $8 students   Subscribers: 12,000

Editorial interest:
    Chronological: unrestricted
    Geographical: Africa, United States, West Indies
    Topical: unrestricted
    Special scope: emphasis on a Black studies perspective

Editorial policies:
    Query and abstract prior to submission of ms.
    Style manual: MLA Style Sheet
    Preferred length of ms.: 20-30 typed pages, longer articles for serialization occasionally accepted
    Author payment: 12 copies of issue in which article appears
    Bottom or end notes. "Authors must be Black. Non-Black authors by invitation only." Accepts mss. in any language, which will be translated if the quality merits it. Publishes in English. Articles should deal with fundamental aspects of the Black experience; can have historical or contemporary emphasis, but should be incisive and stimulating, with a political perspective. One of the important features of the publication is the organization of each issue around a topic of importance such as Black women, Black cities, or Black psychology.

Notes: Book reviews are solicited but freelance offerings are welcome. Preferred length: 500-800 words; remuneration. Reports on submissions in 60 days.

BLACK THEATRE: A Periodical of the Black Theatre Movement

Editor: Ed Bullins

Managing editor: Richard Wesley

Editorial address:
    200 West 135th Street
    Room 103
    Harlem, New York, New York 10030

Sponsor: New Lafayette Theatre

Frequency: irr.   Founded: 1968
Subscription: $5 for 6 issues

Editorial interest:
    Chronological: current events
    Geographical: Africa, Latin America, United States, West Indies
    Topical: anthropology, archaeology, architecture, art, auxiliary historical disciplines, bibliographical articles, cinema and film, communications media, cultural affairs, economics, education, ethnology, folklore, foreign relations, geography, history of ideas, language (philology, semantics), literature (history and criticism), music (history), philosophy, philosophy of history, politics and

> government, religious studies, research methods, science and technology, social history, sociology, theatre and drama
> Special scope: Black art, aesthetics, and theatre

Editorial policies:
> Query prior to submission of ms.
> Author payment: two copies of magazine
> Authors must be Black. Potential authors should write for a Black theatre audience.

Notes: Articles indexed in *Black Theatre*
> Special features: interviews, poetry. Reports on submissions in two weeks.

BLACK WORLD

Executive editor: Hoyt W. Fuller

Associate editor: Carole A. Parks

Editorial address:
> 820 South Michigan Avenue
> Chicago, Illinois 60605

Sponsor: Johnson Publishing Company

Frequency: M
Subscription: $5

Founded: 1942 (as *Negro Digest*)
Circulation: approximately 100,000

Editorial interest:
> Chronological: unrestricted
> Geographical: Africa, Latin America, United States, West Indies
> Topical: anthropology, art, bibliographical articles, cultural affairs, ethnology, folklore, literature (history and criticism), politics and government, social history, theatre and drama
> Special scope: race relations

Editorial policies:
> Query prior to submission of ms.
> Style manual: none prescribed, consult previous issues
> Preferred length of ms.: 3,500 words maximum; longer articles for serialization occasionally accepted
> Author payment: variable cash payment, and two copies of issue in which article appears
> Bottom notes. Accepts mss. and publishes in English. Address mss. to the editors. Potential authors should write for a literate, sophisticated, primarily Black audience.

BLACK WORLD (cont'd)

Notes:

> Special feature: "Perspective," a regular feature of news about artists and the arts. Book reviews are assigned, but freelance offerings are occasionally accepted; cash remuneration. Editorial reports on submissions generally in two weeks.

BULLETIN: British Association of Orientalists

Editor: Jan Knappert

Editorial address
> School of Oriental and African Studies
> University of London
> Mallet Street
> London W.C. 1, England

Sponsor: British Association of Orientalists

Frequency: A

Subscription: £1

Founded: 1946 (as *Bulletin of Oriental Studies*)

Subscribers: 300

Editorial interest:

> Chronological: unrestricted
> Geographical: Asia, East Africa, Middle East, Pacific Area, Russia/USSR
> Topical: anthropology, archaeology, architecture, art, auxiliary historical disciplines, bibliographical articles, education, ethnology, folklore, foreign relations, frontier areas, geography, historiography, history of ideas, international organizations, language (philology, semantics), legal and constitutional affairs, literature (history and criticism), maritime history, medicine (history), music (history), philosophy, philosophy of history, politics and government, religious studies, social history, sociology, theatre and drama

Editorial policies:

> Query prior to submission of ms.
> Style manual: none prescribed, consult previous issues
> Preferred length of ms.: 10-20 typed pages; no serialization
> Author payment: 20 article reprints
> End notes. Contributions from members of the Association are preferred, but submissions by non-members are considered. Potential authors should write for an audience of specialized orientalists.

Notes:

> Special features: philology, bibliography. Full bibliographical references are required, but no illustrations or graphs can be accepted. No book reviews to date. Editorial reports on submissions in six weeks.

BULLETIN DE LA SOCIETE DE GEOGRAPHIE D'EGYPTE

Editor: Mohammed M. Alsayyad

Editorial address:
Société de Géographie d'Egypte
Bureau de Poste
Garden City
Cairo, Arab Republic of Egypt

Sponsor: same as above

Frequency: A
Subscription: ₤4.25, free to members of
the Société

Founded: 1875 (as *Bulletin de
la Société Khediviale de
Géographie*)

Editorial interest:
Chronological: unspecified
Geographical: Africa, Asia, Middle East
Topical: agriculture, anthropology, archaeology, bibliographical articles,
ethnology, frontier areas, geography, historiography, social
history, transportation

Editorial policies:
Query prior to submission of ms.
Style manual: none prescribed, consult previous issues
Preferred length of ms.: 20 typed pages; longer articles accepted for
serialization
Author payment: 45 article reprints
Bottom notes. Accepts mss. and publishes articles in Arabic, English, or
French. Potential authors should write for an audience of pro-
fessional geographers. Wants mss. on geography and related sciences.

Notes: Articles are abstracted in *Bibliographie Géographique International*. No
book reviews. Editorial reports on submissions within a year. Illustrated.

CAHIERS D'ETUDES AFRICAINES

Editorial address:
20 rue de la Baume
75 Paris 8e, France

Sponsor: Ecole Pratique des Hautes Etudes, VIe Section—Sciences Economiques
et Sociales

Frequency: Q
Subscription: 60 Fr

Founded: 1960
Subscribers: approximately
700

Editorial interest:
Chronological: unrestricted
Geographical: Africa
Topical: agriculture, anthropology, archaeology, art, auxiliary historical
disciplines, bibliographical articles, church or ecclesiastical affairs,
cultural affairs, demography, discovery and exploration, economics,

education, ethnology, folklore, foreign relations, frontier areas, geography, historiography, history of ideas, language (philology, semantics), legal and constitutional affairs, literature (history and criticism), military affairs, music (history), politics and government, social history, sociology, theatre and drama
Special scope: economic anthropology, psychology

Editorial policies:
Query prior to submission of ms.
Style manual: Oxford University Press (English), Syndicat des Typographes (French)
Preferred length of ms.: up to 80 typed pages
Author payment: Fr 10 per printed page and 30 article reprints
End notes. Accepts mss. and publishes articles in English or French. Address mss. to Mr. Pierre Alexandre. Potential authors should write for a graduate and post-graduate audience of African specialists.

Notes:
Special feature: research reports. Book reviews are assigned and solicited. Editorial reports on submissions within six months.

CANADIAN JOURNAL OF AFRICAN STUDIES / REVUE CANADIENNE DES ETUDES AFRICAINES

Editors: Michael Mason and Alf Schwarz

Editorial address:
Leacock Building
McGill University
Montreal 110, Quebec, Canada

Sponsor: Canadian Association of African Studies—Association Canadienne des Etudes Africaines

Frequency: TA   Founded: 1967
Subscription: $18   Subscribers: 900

Editorial interest:
Chronological: unrestricted
Geographical: Africa
Topical: unrestricted

Editorial policies:
Style manual: MLA Style Sheet
Preferred length of ms.: 3,000-6,000 words; no serialization
Author payment: 25 article reprints
Bottom notes. Accepts mss. and publishes in English or French. Address English-language mss. to Prof. Myron Echenberg at editorial address. Address French-language mss. to Professeur Alf Schwarz, *La Revue Canadienne des Etudes Africaines*, Université Laval, Québec, P.Q., Canada. Articles should be directed to an academic audience.

CANADIAN JOURNAL OF AFRICAN STUDIES (cont'd)

Notes:
>Special features: "Notes and Documents," which often contains unpublished letters, essays, and mss. that are of value as source material. Book reviews are assigned, but freelance offerings are considered; no remuneration.

CHRONIQUE D'EGYPTE

Editor: Prof. J. Bingen

Editorial address:
>Parc du Cinquantenaire
>1040 Bruxelles
>Belgium

Sponsor: Fondation Egyptologique Reine Elisabeth

Frequency: TA   Founded: 1925
Subscription: BeFr 670

Editorial interest:
>Chronological: unrestricted
>Geographical: Africa, Middle East
>Topical: archaeology, art, bibliographical articles, language (philology)
>Special scope: Egyptology

Editorial policies:
>Articles are accepted and published in French, English, German, or Dutch.

Notes:
>Special features: news and proceedings of the Foundation; "Personalia." Book reviews are assigned and solicited.

CIVILISATIONS

Editorial address:
>Institut National des Civilisations Différentes
>11 Boulevard de Waterloo
>Brussels, Belgium

Sponsor: same as above

Frequency: Q   Founded: 1951
Subscription: BeFr 500

Editorial interest:
>Chronological: unrestricted (tends to emphasize contemporary period)
>Geographical: worldwide
>Topical: agriculture, economics, legal and constitutional affairs, politics and government, social history, sociology
>Special scope: social, political, and economic problems in the evolution of developing ("Third World") countries

CIVILISATIONS (cont'd)

Editorial policies:
> Query prior to submission of ms.
> Style manual: none prescribed
> Preferred length of ms.: 15-20 typed pages; occasionally accepts longer articles for serialization
> Author payment: five copies of issue in which article appears and 20 article reprints
> Bottom notes. Articles published in English and French. Address queries to general secretary.

Notes: Articles abstracted in HA. Authors must send two copies of ms.

COMPARATIVE AND INTERNATIONAL LAW JOURNAL OF SOUTHERN AFRICA

Editors: Allen Copeling, E. R. Harty, and C. H. Muller

Editorial address:
> P.O. Box 392
> Pretoria, South Africa

Sponsors: University of South Africa, General Mining and Finance Corp., Rembrandt Tobacco Co., United Car and Diesel Distributors, and Verloren van Themart Fund for International Law

Frequency: TA

Founded: 1968

Subscription: Rds 9.50

Subscribers: approximately 750

Editorial interest:
> Chronological: unrestricted
> Geographical: worldwide (Southern African emphasis)
> Topical: international law, international organizations, legal and constitutional affairs

Editorial policies:
> Style manual: none prescribed, consult previous issues
> Preferred length of ms.: none; articles accepted for serialization
> Author payment: Rds 2 per printed page, and 20 article reprints
> End notes. Accepts mss. and publishes articles in Afrikaans, Dutch, English (mainly), French, or German. Address mss. to the editors. Wants articles of a suitable academic standard and of general interest.

Notes:
> Special feature: "Current Legal Developments in Southern Africa," which deals with developments in both case and statute law in various African territories. Freelance book review offerings are welcomed; no remuneration. Editorial reports on submissions in approximately four weeks.

CONCH: A Sociological Journal of African Cultures and Literatures

Editor: Sunday O. Anozie

Editorial address:
Department of English
University of Texas
Austin, Texas 78712

Sponsor: Okigbo Friendship Society

Frequency: SA
Subscription: $4/Fr 17.50 individual;
$5.50 institutional

Founded: 1969
Subscribers: 130

Editorial interest:
Chronological: unrestricted
Geographical: Africa, Western Europe
Topical: anthropology, art, bibliographical articles, communications
media, cultural affairs, education, ethnology, folklore, history of
ideas, language (philology, semantics), literature (history and
criticism), music (history), philosophy, religious studies, research
methods, science and technology, sociology, theatre and drama
Special scope: structuralism, theoretical and applied; poetry

Editorial policies:
Style manual: MLA Style Sheet
Preferred length of ms.: 20 typed pages maximum; serialization only on
commissioned articles
Author payment: one copy of issue in which article appears and 10
article reprints
End notes. All articles for annual special September issue are com-
missioned. Accepts mss. and publishes articles in English or
French. Potential authors should write for a scholarly audience.
Wants mss. with thematic unity, clearly and logically written and
documented on structuralism, linguistics, African literature, and
sociology. Also interested in exploratory interdisciplinary studies.

Notes: Articles abstracted or indexed in AES. Potential authors should submit
along with ms. a short biographical note of 60 words for the "Contributors" column. Book reviews are assigned; one copy of issue in which
review appears, and 10 review reprints remuneration. Prospective
reviewers should submit an application to the editor clearly indicating
their field of interest.

CORRESPONDANCE D'ORIENT ETUDES

Editorial address:
44, Avenue Jeanne
1050 Bruxelles

Sponsor: Centre pour l'Etude des Problèmes du Monde Musulman
Contemporain

CORRESPONDANCE D'ORIENT ETUDES (cont'd)

Frequency: A   Founded: 1960
Subscription: BeFr 300   Subscribers: approximately
                                         200

Editorial interest:
> Chronological: 1900 to present, current events
> Geographical: Africa, Asia, Middle East
> Topical: bibliographical articles, cultural affairs, economics, education,
> ethnology, foreign relations, geography, historiography, history
> of ideas, language (philology, semantics), legal and constitutional
> affairs, literature (history and criticism), philosophy of history,
> politics and government, religious studies, social history, sociology
> Special scope: contemporary Muslim world

Editorial policies:
> Publishes articles in French and English. No other data reported.

Notes:
> Special features: "Activities of the Center." Book reviews are assigned
> and solicited.

CRICKET

Editors: Imamu Amiri Baraka, Larry Neal, and Ab Spellman

Editorial address:
> Box 663
> Newark, New Jersey 07101

Sponsor: Jihad Productions

Frequency: BM   Founded: 1968
Subscription: $2

Editorial interest:
> Chronological: unrestricted
> Geographical: Africa, United States, West Indies
> Topical: art, communications media, cultural affairs, music (history),
> theatre and drama
> Special scope: Black music in evolution and Africans everywhere

Editorial policies:
> Author payment: no cash at the moment, copies of issue on request
> Accepts and publishes articles in English or Swahili. Mss. should be sent
> to Jeledi Katibu, Managing Editor. Would like to see "articles that
> offer alternatives to racism that exists, through creation of Black
> institutions."

CRISIS: A Record of the Darker Races

Editor: Henry Lee Moon

Editorial address:
 1790 Broadway
 New York, New York 10019

Sponsor: National Association for the Advancement of Colored People

Frequency: 10 xy
Subscription: $3.50

Founded: 1910
Subscribers: 100,000

Editorial interest:
 Chronological: unrestricted
 Geographical: Africa, Canada, United States, West Indies
 Topical: anthropology, archaeology, art, auxiliary historical disciplines,
  cultural affairs, foreign relations, history of ideas, international
  organizations, language (philology, semantics), philosophy of
  history, politics and government, social history, sociology, theatre
  and drama
 Special scope: Negro life and history

Editorial policies:
 Query prior to submission of ms.
 Style manual: none prescribed
 Preferred length of ms.: 2,000-3,000 words; accepts longer articles for
  serialization
 Author payment: six article reprints; sometimes more upon request
 No notes. Accepts mss. and publishes articles in English. Potential authors
  should write for an audience interested in civil rights, Negro life,
  culture, and history. Welcomes mss. in history, biography, African affairs, and culture of non-White groups, particularly of Black
  folk; civil rights struggle; each article, poem or short story should
  deal with these subjects.

Notes: Articles abstracted or cited in AHL and HA. Book reviews normally
 assigned, but freelance reviews considered; no remuneration. Reports on
 submissions vary from one week to several months, "depending on work-
 load in the office."

CURRENT BIBLIOGRAPHY ON AFRICAN AFFAIRS

Editor: Daniel G. Matthews

Editorial address:
 P.O. Box 13096
 Washington, D.C. 20009

Sponsor: African Bibliographical Center

Frequency: BM
Subscription: $25

Founded: 1963

CURRENT BIBLIOGRAPHY ON AFRICAN AFFAIRS (cont'd)

Editorial interest:
> Chronological: unrestricted
> Geographical: Africa, Latin America, Middle East, United States,
> > West Indies
> Topical: unrestricted

Editorial policies:
> Query prior to submission of ms.
> Style manual: Chicago
> Preferred length of ms.: 2,000-6,000 words; accepts longer articles for
> > serialization
> Author payment: 25 article reprints
> Bottom or end notes. Accepts mss. and publishes articles in English or
> > French. Potential authors should write for an academic or library
> > world audience. All submissions, whether general or specialized in
> > scope, should be well documented.

Notes: Articles abstracted or indexed in *Africa: Index of the International
> *African Institute*, *American Geographical Society*, PAIS
> Special feature: annotated bibliographical information. Book reviews are
> > assigned, but freelance offerings are considered; no remuneration.

DAILY NEWS—SUNDAY NEWS

Editor: Ben Mkapa

Editorial address:
> P.O. Box 9033
> Dar Es Salaam, Tanzania

Sponsor: government owned

Frequency: Daily-Sunday-Weekly   Founded: Daily, 1930;
> > Sunday, 1954

Editorial interest:
> Chronological: current events, unrestricted
> Geographical: worldwide
> Topical: agriculture, economics, education, foreign relations, politics
> > and government, theatre and drama, transportation

Editorial policies:
> Style manual: none prescribed
> Preferred length of ms.: 1,000 words
> Author payment: negotiated
> Authors should direct their material toward an audience comprised
> > largely of the "workers and peasants of Tanzania." Would like to
> > see articles of " . . . all kinds, (which) should be straightforward;
> > . . . we prefer those which help our people to carry on the war
> > against imperialism, colonialism, capitalism, etc."

Notes: Book reviews "usually assigned, but we accept freelance offers if they help out the liberation struggle." Editorial reports on submissions usually take several weeks.

DEVELOPMENT AND CHANGE

Editors: M. Doornbos, Kurt Martin, H. Linnemann, and F. Wils

Assistant editor: J. Sanders

Editorial address:
Institute of Social Studies
Molenstraat 27
The Hague, Netherlands

Sponsor: same as above

Frequency: TA   Founded: 1969
Subscription: Dfl 30

Editorial interest:
Chronological: unspecified
Geographical: Africa, Asia, Latin America, Middle East, West Indies
Topical: unrestricted (if related to development)
Special scope: development

Editorial policies:
Query prior to submission of ms.
Style manual: none prescribed
Preferred length of ms.: 4,000-5,000 words; no serialization
Author payment: 24 article reprints
Bottom notes. Address mss. to the assistant editor. Potential contributors should write for social scientists concerned with the problems of developing countries. Wants provocative, original, well-researched mss. on all phases of development.

Notes:
Special features: commentaries and reports. Book reviews are assigned and solicited, but freelance offerings are considered; no remuneration. Editorial reports on submissions in approximately one month.

DRUM

Editor: Olu Adetule (Nigeria)

Editorial addresses:
Drum Publications (U.K.) Limited
40-43 Fleet Street
London, E.C. 4, England
Cables: "Drumbeats" London

DRUM (cont'd)

Drum Publications (Nigeria) Limited
37 Ibadan Street West
Ebute Metta
P.M.G. 2128, Lagos
Cables: "Drumbeats"

Drum Publications (Ghana) Limited
House F219/2
Corner of Abrebrensem Street
Osu (Christiansborg)
P.O. Box 1197
Accra
Cables: "Drumbeats"

Drum Publications (E.A.) Limited
Mutual Building
Kimathi Street
P.O. Box 3372
Nairobi, Kenya
Cables: "Drumbeats"

Frequency: M
Cover price: 1s.6d

Founded: 1951
Circulation: 520,000

Editorial interest:
Chronological: unrestricted
Geographical: unrestricted, with an emphasis upon Pan-Africa
Topical: unrestricted

Editorial policies:
Drum is a popular magazine that maintains its own editorial staff
throughout Africa. Rarely seeks freelance contributions.

Notes: Companion magazine, *Trust* (founded 1971; circulation 145,000),
edited in Nigeria by Mr. Adetule.

EAST AFRICA JOURNAL

Editor: Allan Bethwill Ogot

Managing editor: Richard Carl Ntiru

Editorial address:
P.O. Box 30492
Nairobi, Kenya

Sponsor: East African Cultural Trust

Frequency: M
Subscription: 30 East African shillings, $10
outside Africa

Founded: 1964
Subscribers: 1,757

EAST AFRICA JOURNAL (cont'd)

Editorial interest:
>Chronological: unrestricted
>
>Geographical: Africa (mostly), Asia, Latin America, Middle East
>
>Topical: cultural affairs, economics, education, history of ideas, literature (history and criticism), politics and government, sociology
>
>Special scope: developments in the Third World, especially Africa; exploration of space

Editorial policies:
>Style manual: any
>
>Preferred length of ms.: 3,000 words maximum; longer articles for serialization considered
>
>Author payment: two copies of issue in which article appears
>
>Notes discouraged; if they are necessary, they should be integrated in text. Accepts mss. and publishes articles in English. Address mss. to managing editor. Potential authors should write for those who are in positions to affect public developmental policies. Wants mss. on cultural, economic, political, and social developments in the Third World, especially Africa.

Notes:
>Special feature: monthly list of titles of books published in Africa. Book reviews are assigned and solicited, but freelance offerings are considered if work is relevant to Africa or the Third World. Preferred length of book reviews: 800 words. Persons interested in reviewing should contact the managing editor. Editorial reports on submissions within 20 days.

EAST AFRICAN AGRICULTURAL AND FORESTRY JOURNAL

Editor: Tecwyn Jones

Editorial address:
>East African Agriculture and Forestry Research Organization
>P.O. Box 30148
>Nairobi, Kenya

Sponsor: East African Community

Frequency: Q

Founded: 1935

Subscription: 25s in East Africa; $7/ £2.5/ DM25 elsewhere

Subscribers: 1,000

Editorial interest:
>Chronological: current events
>
>Geographical: Africa
>
>Topical: agriculture
>
>Special scope: ecology, forestry, fisheries, wildlife

EAST AFRICAN AGRICULTURAL AND FORESTRY JOURNAL (cont'd)

Editorial policies:
>Query prior to submission of ms.
>Style manual: "Rules and Notes for the Guidance of Authors" on the inside cover of each issue
>Preferred length of ms.: unspecified
>Author payment: 25 article reprints
>Bottom notes. Accepts mss. and publishes articles in English. Wants original, scientific papers dealing with research in agriculture, forestry, fisheries, veterinary medicine, animal husbandry, entomology, pathology, virology, plant genetics, and wildlife

Notes: Articles are abstracted or indexed in CC, *Forestry Abstracts* (UK), *Entomological Abstracts* (UK). Book reviews are assigned; no remuneration. Editorial reports on submissions within one to four weeks.

EAST AFRICAN GEOGRAPHICAL REVIEW

Editors: R. T. Jackson and B. W. Langlands

Editorial address:
>Department of Geography
>Makerere University
>P.O. Box 7062
>Kampala, Uganda

Sponsor: Uganda Geographical Association

Frequency: A

Subscription: 25 East African shillings in East Africa; 30 East African shillings elsewhere

Founded: 1963

Subscribers: approximately 850

Editorial interest:
>Chronological: unrestricted, but mainly 1900 to present
>Geographical: Africa, East Africa (mainly)
>Topical: agriculture, anthropology, bibliographical articles, discovery and exploration, economics, ethnology, frontier areas, geography, maritime history, research methods, transportation
>Special scope: economic development in tropical areas

Editorial policies:
>Query prior to submission of ms. optional
>Style manual: any
>Preferred length of ms.: 1,500-4,500 words for the "Records" section, 4,500-9,000 words for articles
>Author payment: 15 article reprints
>End notes. Accepts English-, French-, Luganda-, and Swahili-language mss. Publishes articles in English or possibly Swahili. Potential authors should write for an international audience of geographers and East African geography teachers. Wants authoritative mss. on East Africa, French-speaking Africa—Congo, Gabon, Centafrique, etc.—and Angola and Mozambique.

EAST AFRICAN GEOGRAPHICAL REVIEW (cont'd)

Notes: Articles cited in Chauncy Harris, *Guide to Geographical Periodicals*,
Royal Geographical Society, *New Periodicals and Maps*, SSHI.
Special feature: "Research Record," which deals with current geographical research in East Africa. Book reviews are assigned and solicited, but freelance offerings are accepted; no remuneration. Editorial reports on submissions generally within one month.

EASTERN AFRICA ECONOMIC REVIEW

Editor: J. K. Maitha

Editorial address:
Department of Economics
University of Nairobi
P.O. Box 30197
Nairobi, Kenya

Sponsors: University of Nairobi; University of Dar es Salaam; Makerere University, Kampala; University of Kharoum; University of Zambia and the Economic Club of Kenya

Frequency: SA
Subscription: £2 in United Kingdom;
$5 elsewhere

Founded: 1953 (as *East African Economic Review*, name changed 1969)
Subscribers: approximately 500

Editorial interest:
Chronological: 1900 to present, current events
Geographical: Africa, East Africa
Topical: economics
Special scope: problems of developing economies

Editorial policies:
Query prior to submission of ms. optional
Style manual: Oxford University Press format, "Notes for the Guidance of Authors" available on request
Preferred length of ms.: 3,000-7,000 words; accepts longer articles for serialization
Author payment: 25 article reprints
End notes. Accepts mss. and publishes articles in English. Potential authors should write for an international audience of professional economists. Wants mss. on the economic problems in developing African nations, particularly East African.

Notes: Articles abstracted in JEL. Authors should submit the original and one copy of the ms., typed, double-spaced on quarto size paper. Book reviews are assigned; no remuneration. Persons interested in reviewing should contact Dr. S. M. Mbilinyi, Book Review Editor, University of Dar es Salaam, P.O. Box 35051, Dar es Salaam, Tanzania. Editorial reports on submissions within one to three months after the acknowledgment of receipt of the ms. by the editor.

EASTERN AFRICA LAW REVIEW: A Journal of Law and Development

Editor: I. G. Shivji

Associate editors: F. M. Kassan and A. R. Lyall

Editorial address:
Faculty of Law
University of Dar es Salaam
P.O. Box 35093
Dar es Salaam, Tanzania

Sponsor: same as above

Frequency: TA
Subscription: 50 Tanzanian shillings individual in East Africa; 60 Tanzanian shillings individual outside

Founded: 1968
Subscribers: 800

Editorial interest:
Chronological: unrestricted
Geographical: worldwide
Topical: international law, international organizations, legal and constitutional affairs, research methods
Special scope: development

Editorial policies:
Style manual: any
Preferred length of ms.: 25-40 typed pages; longer articles for serialization occasionally considered
Author payment: one copy of issue in which article appears and 20 article reprints
Bottom notes. Accepts mss. and publishes articles in English. Address mss. to the editor. Potential authors should write for an audience of lawyers and social scientists. Wants mss. on law and development.

Notes:
Special features: notes and comments on decided cases. Book reviews are assigned and solicited, but freelance offerings are considered. Persons interested in reviewing should contact the editor. Editorial reports on submissions in about three months.

ECONOMIC BULLETIN OF GHANA

Editor: J. C. de Graft-Johnson

Editorial address:
P.O. Box 22
Legon, Ghana

Sponsor: Economic Society of Ghana

Frequency: Q
Subscription: NL 5.50

Founded: 1957
Subscribers: 517

ECONOMIC BULLETIN OF GHANA (cont'd)

Editorial interest:
    Chronological: unspecified
    Geographical: Africa
    Topical: economics

Editorial policies:
    Style manual: none prescribed
    Preferred length of ms.: 15-30 typed pages; longer articles accepted for
        serialization
    Author payment: 30 article reprints
    End notes. Accepts mss. and publishes articles in English. Potential
        authors should write for an audience interested in African economic
        issues.

Notes: Articles indexed in SSHI. Potential contributors should submit the
    original and at least one copy of the ms. Book reviews are assigned and
    solicited; no remuneration. Editorial reports on submissions in about
    three months.

ENGLISH STUDIES IN AFRICA

Editor: Brian Cheadle

Editorial address:
    Publications Officer
    Witwatersrand University Press
    Jan Smuts Avenue
    Johannesburg, South Africa

Sponsor: same as above

Frequency: SA   Founded: 1958
Subscription: Rds 3   Subscribers: approximately
                                        250

Editorial interest:
    Chronological: unrestricted
    Geographical: Africa
    Topical: education, language (philology, semantics), literature (history
        and criticism), philosophy, theatre and drama

Editorial policies:
    Style manual: "W.U.P. House Style" is available on request
    Preferred length of ms.: 25 typed quarto size pages; no serialization
    Author payment: none, except in the case of professional writers;
        Rds 2.10 for 500 words, with a minimum of Rds 6.30 and a maxi-
        mum of Rds 21 per article; 12 article reprints to all authors
    Accepts mss. and publishes articles in English. Articles should be
        scholarly. Wants mss. of a literary and critical nature.

ENGLISH STUDIES IN AFRICA (cont'd)

Notes: Cited or abstracted in APS, HA, LLBA. Potential contributors should note that all long quotations should be indented and reference notes should be numbered consecutively. Book reviews are solicited; no remuneration. Editorial decision on submissions in two to three months.

ESSENCE: Magazine for Today's Black Woman

Editor-in-chief: Marcia Ann Gillespie

Executive editor: Sheila Younge

Copy editor: Edmonia D. Watkins

Fiction/poetry/books editor: Sharyn J. Skeeter

Editorial address:
300 East 42nd Street
New York, New York 10017

Sponsor: Hollingsworth Group

Frequency: M   Founded: 1970
Subscription: $6   Subscribers: 2,800

Editorial interest:
Chronological: unrestricted
Geographical: Africa, Latin America, United States (mainly), West Indies, Western Europe
Topical: unrestricted
Special scope: fiction, poetry, which are of current interest to Black women

Editorial policies:
Query letter preferred but not necessary. For specific information concerning mss. send query to appropriate editor.
Style manual: Chicago
Preferred length of ms.: maximum of 20 pages, longer articles for serialization occasionally accepted
Author payment: $150-$500 and one copy of issue in which article appears
Bottom or end notes, as few as possible. Accepts mss. generally in English only. Address non-fiction mss. to editor-in-chief, fiction and poetry mss. to fiction/poetry/books editor. Articles should "not necessarily be slanted. However, the audience—Black women—should be kept in mind. Open to all feature-length articles of current interest."

Notes:
Special features: consumer advice, medical information, recreation. Book reviews are staff written. Editorial reports on submissions in one to eight weeks.

ETHIOPIAN GEOGRAPHICAL JOURNAL

Editor: Hailu Wolde Emmanuel

Editorial address:
Imperial Ethiopian Government Mapping and Geography Institute
P.O. Box 597
Addis Ababa, Ethiopia

Sponsor: same as above

Frequency: SA
Subscription: $2

Founded: 1963
Subscribers: 700

Editorial interest:
Chronological: unrestricted
Geographical: Africa, Ethiopia
Topical: agriculture, anthropology, archaeology, bibliographical
articles, communications media, cultural affairs, demography,
discovery and exploration, economics, geography

Editorial policies:
Style manual: none prescribed
Preferred length of ms.: 4,000-8,000 words; accepts longer articles for
serialization
Author payment: 20 or more article reprints
Bottom notes. Accepts mss. and publishes articles in Amharic or
English. Potential authors should write for a university-educated
professional audience. Wants mss. on the natural and human
resources of Ethiopia, Ethiopian regional studies, and mapping.

Notes: Abstracted or indexed in *Annotated World List of Selected Current
Geographical Serials in English, Current Geographical Publications.*
Book reviews are solicited; no remuneration. Editorial reports on sub-
missions in about three months.

ETHIOPIAN OBSERVER

Editors: Richard Pankhurst and Rita Pankhurst

Editorial address:
P.O. Box 1896
Addis Ababa, Ethiopia

Frequency: Q
Subscription: £1.10

Founded: 1936 (as *New
Times and Ethiopia
News*; name changed
1956)
Subscribers: 3,000

Editorial interest:
Chronological: 1100 to present, current events
Geographical: Africa, Ethiopia
Topical: agriculture, anthropology, archaeology, architecture, art,
auxiliary historical disciplines, bibliographical articles,

ETHIOPIAN OBSERVER (cont'd)

communications media, cultural affairs, discovery and exploration, economics, education, ethnology, folklore, foreign relations, geography, historiography, international law, military affairs, music (history), social history, sociology

Editorial policies:
Query letter prior to submission of ms. optional
Style manual: none prescribed
Preferred length of ms.: 50 typed pages
Author payment: six article reprints
Accepts mss. and publishes articles in English.

Notes: Persons interested in book reviewing should contact the editors; no remuneration. Editorial reports on submissions in one month.

ETHNOS

Editors: Bengt Danielsson and Olga Olofsson

Editorial address:
Ethnografiska Museet
115 27 Stockholm, Sweden

Frequency: A
Subscription: Scr 30

Founded: 1936
Subscribers: approximately
500

Editorial interest:
Chronological: unrestricted
Geographical: Africa, Asia, Australia, Latin America, Middle East, Pacific Area, West Indies
Topical: anthropology, archaeology, art, discovery and exploration, ethnology, folklore, language (philology, semantics), maritime history, music (history), research methods, science and technology, sociology

Editorial policies:
Style manual: none prescribed
Preferred length of ms.: 3-15 typed pages; rarely accepts longer articles for serialization
Author payment: 25 article reprints
Bottom notes. Accepts mss. and publishes articles in English, French, or Spanish. Potential authors should write for an international audience interested in anthropology, archaeology, and music.

Notes: Articles indexed in SSHI. Mss. must be typed, without corrections, and ready for the press. Book reviews are assigned and solicited; no remuneration. Persons interested in reviewing should contact the editors. Editorial reports on submissions in two to four weeks.

FOCUS: Magazine of the Students of the University of Science and Technology

Editors: I. A. Doku, Johnnie Amnah, S. K. Gakpo, Miss Gertrude Mensah, and I. B. Ohene

Editorial address:
S.R.C. Office
University of Science and Technology
Kumasi, Ghana

Sponsor: Students Representative Council of the University of Science and Technology

Frequency: SA   Founded: 1969
Subscription: Cedi 1.20

Editorial interest:
Chronological: unrestricted
Geographical: worldwide
Topical: unrestricted

Editorial policies:
Style manual: none prescribed
Preferred length of ms.: 25 typed pages; serialization acceptable
Author payment: one copy of issue in which article appears
Bottom notes. Accepts mss. and publishes articles in English. Wants mss. on student power activities.

Notes:
Special features: "News from Campus." No book reviews. Editorial decision on submissions in one week.

FOLIA ORIENTALIA

Editor: F. Machalski

Editorial address:
Cracow
Al. Mickiewicza 9/11, Poland

Sponsor: Polish Academy of Sciences, Cracow Section

Frequency: A   Founded: 1959
Subscription: varies

Editorial interest:
Chronological: unrestricted
Geographical: Africa, Asia, Middle East
Topical: anthropology, archaeology, art, folklore, historiography, language (philology, semantics), literature (history and criticism)

Editorial policies:
Preferred length of ms.: 20-30 typed pages
Author payment: cash payment varies; approximately 20 to 25 complimentary reprints of article

FOLIA ORIENTALIA (cont'd)

End notes. Accepts mss. in "any better known language with no rare alphabet." (The exception is Arabic, for which there are printing facilities.) Publishes in English, French, German, and occasionally other languages. Would like to see articles primarily concerning languages and literatures of the Middle East, ancient and modern, and Africa.

Notes: Articles are abstracted or indexed in *Abstracta Islamica, Afrika und Ubersee*. All relevant books for reviewing should be sent to the editor; freelance book reviews are accepted. Reports on submissions in three to four months.

FORUM

Editor: Agyare Koillarbi

Editorial address: Students Representative Council
University of Ghana
Legon, Accara, Ghana

Sponsor: same as above

Frequency: M   Founded: 1970
Subscription: $5

Editorial interest:
Chronological: current events
Geographical: Africa
Topical: unrestricted

Editorial policies:
Query letter prior to submission of ms. optional
Style manual: none prescribed
Preferred length of ms.: 10 typed pages maximum; no serialization
Author payment: one copy of issue in which article appears
Accepts mss. and publishes in English. Wants mss. that deal with political and scientific developments with particular reference to emerging nations. Articles must be objective and free from all kinds of prejudice.

Notes: Book reviews are assigned and solicited, but freelance offerings are considered. Editorial reports on submissions within three weeks.

THE FORUM

Editor: Clarence E. Eastmond

Editorial address:
1064 Fulton Street
Brooklyn, New York 11238

Sponsor: African-American Teachers Association, Inc.

THE FORUM (cont'd)

Frequency: 10 xy Founded: 1965
Subscription: $5 Subscribers: 2,000

Editorial interest:
Chronological: unrestricted
Geographical: Africa, Latin America, United States, West Indies
Topical: art, education, literature (history and criticism), music (history), social history

Editorial policies:
No restrictions on length of ms.; longer articles accepted for serialization
Author payment: 12 complimentary article reprints
End notes. Editor emphasizes, "Be positive" in preparing the ms.

Notes:
Special features: art and photography. No book reviews. Reports on submissions in two weeks.

FREEDOMWAYS: A Quarterly Journal of the Freedom Movement

Managing editor: Esther Jackson

Associate editors: John H. Clarke, Ernest Kaiser, and John O'Dell

Editorial address:
799 Broadway
New York, New York 10003

Sponsor: Freedomways Associates, Inc.

Frequency: Q Founded: 1961
Subscription: $4.50 U.S.; $6 other areas Subscribers: approximately 8,000

Editorial interest:
Chronological: unrestricted (emphasis on periods of special interest to Afro-Americans and people of African descent)
Geographical: Africa, Asia, Canada, Eastern Europe, Latin America, Middle East, Russia/USSR, United States, West Indies
Topical: anthropology, art, communications media, cultural affairs, economics, literature (history and criticism), politics and government, sociology, theatre and drama

Editorial policies:
Query prior to submission of ms.
Style manual: none prescribed
Preferred length of ms.: unrestricted; does not usually accept articles for serialization
Author payment: 10 copies of magazine in which article appears
End notes. Address mss. or correspondence to managing editor.

FREEDOMWAYS (cont'd)

Notes: Articles cited or abstracted in *Black Information Index, CCM Information Index, Current Index to Journals in Education, Index to Periodical Articles By and About Negroes* (G. K. Hall, Boston).

Special features: recent book listings in addition to book reviews, poetry, art. Book reviews usually assigned; reviewers receive copies of magazine in which review appears. Reports on submissions in 90 days.

GHANA JOURNAL OF EDUCATION

Editor: E. K. Baah-Gyimah

Supervising editor: S. A. A. Djoleto

Editorial address:
Ministry of Education
P.O. Box M45
Accra, Ghana

Sponsor: Ghana government through the Ministry of Education

Frequency: Q
Subscription: $7.40

Founded: 1969, in its present form

Editorial interest:
Chronological: current events
Geographical: Africa
Topical: education, research methods
Special scope: any subject from both local and foreign sources that will be of use in the educational advancement of Ghana

Editorial policies:
Preferred length of ms.: 1,500 to 3,000 words; longer articles considered for serialization
Author payment: five copies of issue in which article appears
Bottom notes preferred. Publishes articles in English, French, or, to some extent, local languages. Articles should be written for an audience of professional teachers and educators. Would especially like to see articles on education in general, with special reference to pre-university education. However, readable and intelligible papers and articles from other educational research sources would be welcome. Articles should improve educational practice in Ghana, expose new ideas on education, and highlight research work in education that will be relevant to the Ghana situation.

Notes:
Special feature: "Pedagogy." Book reviews are solicited; freelance offerings are accepted. Reports on submissions in about three months.

HARVARD JOURNAL OF AFRO-AMERICAN AFFAIRS

Editor: Lee A. Daniels

Editorial address:
20 Sacramento Street
Cambridge, Massachusetts 02138

Sponsor: Harvard-Radcliffe Afro-American Cultural Center

Frequency: SA
Subscription: $2.50

Founded: 1965 (as *Harvard Journal of Negro Affairs*)
Subscribers: 1,500

Editorial interest:
Chronological: unrestricted
Geographical: Africa, Canada, Latin America, United States, West Indies
Topical: unrestricted
Special scope: the Black experience, historical and contemporary, poetry

Editorial policies:
Query prior to submission of ms. optional
Style manual: none prescribed
Preferred length of ms.: 10-20 typed pages; accepts longer articles for serialization
Author payment: none
Bottom or end notes. Prefers English-language mss. Publishes articles in English. Potential authors should write for an audience that is interested or aware of the Black experience. Seeks mss., including poetry, that explore subjects of concern to Black people; the kinds of mss. sought are open-ended.

Notes: Freelance offerings of book reviews are welcomed; no remuneration. Editorial reports on submissions within one month.

HOWARD LAW JOURNAL

Editor-in-chief: Gilbert T. Ray

Editorial address:
Howard University
School of Law
6th and Howard Place, N.W.
Washington, D.C. 20001

Sponsor: Howard University School of Law

Frequency: Q
Subscription: $6

Founded: 1955
Subscribers: 800

Editorial interest:
Chronological: current events, occasional historical articles
Geographical: Africa, United States, West Indies

HOWARD LAW JOURNAL (cont'd)

Topical: business, international organizations, legal and constitutional affairs, politics and government

Editorial policies:

Style manual: none prescribed, consult previous issues

Preferred length of ms.: none; serialization acceptable

Author payment: 25 article reprints

Bottom or end notes. Desires mss. concerning developments in American law and their effects on minority people. "The critical factors in our determination of whether an article will be published are the treatment given the subject matter and the currency of the subject matter."

Notes: Cited in ILP

Special features: "Note" and "Recent Development" columns, which contain student-written and -edited articles. Book reviews are assigned and solicited. Persons interested in reviewing should contact book review editor at the editorial address. Editorial decision on offerings within three weeks.

IBADAN: Journal of the University

Editor: T. Adesanya Ige Goillo

Editorial address:
University of Ibadan
Ibadan, Nigeria

Sponsor: same as above

Frequency: SA

Subscription: $2/15s

Founded: 1957

Subscribers: approximately 600

Editorial interest:

Chronological: unrestricted

Geographical: Africa

Topical: unrestricted

Special scope: poetry, interdisciplinary African studies

Editorial policies:

Query prior to submission of ms. optional

Style manual: any

Preferred length of ms.: unrestricted

Author payment: 25 article reprints

Bottom or end notes. Accepts mss. and publishes articles in English and any Nigerian language. Potential authors should write for a university level audience. Wants mss. on African studies, current African affairs, educational methodology, history, language, poetry, or sociology.

IBADAN (cont'd)

Notes: Articles abstracted or indexed in CC, HA, SSHI. Book reviews are assigned, but freelance offerings are considered if pertinent to Nigeria or Africa; no remuneration. Editorial reports on submissions in two to three months.

INSIGHT AND OPINION

Editorial executive: K. O. Amoah

Editor: Kojo Bentsi-Enchill

Editorial address:
Nananom Publishers
P.O. Box 5446
Accra North, Ghana

Frequency: Q
Subscription: $7

Founded: 1965
Subscribers: 2,000

Editorial interest:
Chronological: unrestricted
Geographical: Africa (mainly) and other areas if related to Africa
Topical: unrestricted

Editorial policies:
Query prior to submission of ms. optional
Style manual: none prescribed
Preferred length of ms.: 2,000-5,000 words; longer articles for serialization accepted
Author payment: cash remuneration rate and subject to negotiation, and two copies of issues in which article appears
End notes. Accepts English-, and French-language mss. Publishes in English. Potential authors should write for a cultivated, intellectual, wide-ranging audience.

Notes: Book reviews are assigned, but freelance offerings are welcome; remuneration possible. Editorial reports on submissions in two to four weeks.

INSTITUTE FOR THE STUDY OF MAN IN AFRICA

Secretary: Mrs. E. Hibbert

Editorial address:
Institute for the Study of Man in Africa
Medical School
University of Witwatersrand
Hospital Street
Johannesburg, South Africa

Sponsor: same as above

INSTITUTE FOR THE STUDY OF MAN IN AFRICA (cont'd)

Frequency: irr.
Subscription: Rds 4/£2 individual;
    Rds 1/10s students; Rds 5/£2
    institutional

Founded: 1961
Subscribers: approximately
    500

Editorial interest:
    Chronological: unrestricted
    Geographical: Africa
    Topical: anthropology, archaeology, art, bibliographical articles,
        cultural affairs, demography, economics, education, folklore,
        medicine (history), music (history), religious studies, social his-
        tory, sociology
    Special scope: migration, race relations, tribalism

Editorial policies:
    The publications of the Institute consist of monthly lectures and an
    Annual Raymond Dart Lecture.

INSTITUTE OF DEVELOPMENT STUDIES BULLETIN

Editors: Clive Bell and Dudley Seers

Editorial address:
    Institute of Development Studies
    Andrew Cohen Building
    University of Sussex
    Falmer, Brighton BN1 9RE, England

Sponsor: same as above

Frequency: Q
Subscription: £1/$2.50

Founded: 1969
Circulation: 2,800

Editorial interest:
    Chronological: 1900 to present (current emphasis)
    Geographical: worldwide (stresses underdeveloped countries)
    Topical: business, cultural affairs, economics, foreign relations, frontier
        areas, geography, international organizations, politics and govern-
        ment, research methods, science and technology, social history,
        sociology
    Special scope: interdisciplinary development studies

Editorial policies:
    Query prior to submission of ms. is advised, since each issue is devoted
        to a central theme
    Style manual: none prescribed
    Preferred length of ms.: 3,000 words
    Author payment: 25 article reprints
    Address correspondence to the editor. Interested in scholarly articles
        that are timely and that are free of jargon and unnecessary
        footnotes.

INTERNATIONAL JOURNAL OF AFRICAN HISTORICAL STUDIES

Editor: Norman R. Bennett

Editorial address:
10 Lenox Street
Brookline, Massachusetts 02146

Sponsor: African Studies Center, Boston University

Frequency: TA
Subscription: $15 individual; $20
institutional

Founded: 1968 (as *African Historical Studies*)
Subscribers: 500

Editorial interest:
Chronological: unrestricted
Geographical: Africa
Topical: archaeology, auxiliary historical disciplines, discovery and exploration, foreign relations, historiography, history of ideas, legal and constitutional affairs, literature (history), maritime history, philosophy of history, politics and government, research methods, science and technology, social history
Special scope: all historical topics relating to Africa

Editorial policies:
Style manual: Kate L. Turabian, *A Manual for Writers*
Preferred length of ms.: unrestricted; accepts long articles for serialization
Author payment: none
End notes. Accepts mss. and publishes articles in English or French; may consider other languages in the future. Potential authors should write for an audience interested in Africa's past.

Notes: Articles abstracted or indexed in *Africa, African Abstracts, American Historical Review*, HA. Book reviews are solicited, but freelance offerings are considered; no remuneration.

ISLAM: Zeitschrift für Geschichte und Kultur des islamischen Orients

Editor: Bertold Spuler

Editorial address:
Seminar für Geschichte und Kultur des Vorden Orients
University of Hamburg
Rothenbaumchaussee 36
2 Hamburg 13, Federal Republic of Germany

Sponsor: same as above

Frequency: SA
Subscription: DM 64

Founded: 1910
Subscribers: approximately 300

Editorial interest:
Chronological: 622 to the present

ISLAM (cont'd)

Geographical: Africa, Asia, Balkans, Iberia, Middle East (mainly), Pacific Area, Russia/USSR (Islamic areas only)

Topical: anthropology, architecture, art, auxiliary historical disciplines, cultural affairs, education, ethnology, geography, historiography, history of ideas, language (philology, semantics), literature (history and criticism), medicine (history), music (history), philosophy, philosophy of history, religious studies

Special scope: Islamic civilization

Editorial policies:

Style manual: advisory leaf for authors available on request

Preferred length of ms.: 20 typed pages; accepts longer articles for serialization

Author payment: 25 article reprints

End notes. Accepts mss. and publishes articles in English, French, or German. Wants mss. on all topics relevant to the understanding of Islamic civilization.

Notes:

Special feature: personalia. Book reviews are assigned and solicited. Editorial reports on submissions as soon as possible.

JOURNAL OF AFRICAN HISTORY

Editors: A. G. Hopkins, R. C. C. Law, S. Marks, and A. D. Roberts

Editorial address:
School of Oriental and African Studies
University of London
London W.C.1, England

Sponsor: Cambridge University Press

Frequency: Q

Subscription: £7/$23

Founded: 1960

Subscribers: approximately 3,000

Editorial interest:
Chronological: unrestricted
Geographical: Africa
Topical: archaeology
Special scope: history

Editorial policies:
Style manual: "Contributions" printed on back inside cover of journal
Preferred length of ms.: 5,000-6,000 words; no serialization
Author payment: 25 article reprints
Bottom notes. Accepts mss. and publishes articles in English or French. Potential authors should write for specialists in African history, but not for specialists in the same region of Africa as themselves. Wants articles that embody the results of original research.

JOURNAL OF AFRICAN HISTORY (cont'd)

Notes: Articles abstracted or indexed in *British Humanities Index*, HA, SSHI. Authors should submit two copies of ms., double-spaced on quarto paper. Book reviews are assigned, but freelance offerings are considered on their merits; space limitations for the Review Section are strict.

JOURNAL OF AFRICAN LANGUAGES

Editor: Irvine Richardson

Editorial address:
Center for International Programs
Michigan State University
East Lansing, Michigan 48823

Sponsor: same as above

Frequency: TA   Founded: 1962
Subscription: $9/£3   Subscribers: 300

Editorial interest:
Chronological: unrestricted
Geographical: Africa
Topical: language (linguistics)

Editorial policies:
Query prior to submission of ms.
Style manual: any
Preferred length of ms.: varies, generally 5,000-10,000 words; accepts longer articles for serialization
Author payment: 25 article reprints
End notes. Accepts mss. and publishes articles in English, French, or German. Potential authors should write for university staff, post-graduate, and equivalent levels. Wants mss. on linguistics (including socio-, and psycho-linguistics; branches such as phonetics, syntax, morphology), preferably analytical and critical studies.

Notes: Potential authors should submit original and one copy of ms., typed, double-spaced with wide margins. Language data must be italicized in inverted commas. Material author wishes to be underlined should be marked "underline" in margin. Illustrations, maps, etc., should be submitted with ms. Reviews are normally assigned; off-prints for remuneration. Persons interested in reviewing should contact the review editor, Dr. Gordon Innes, School of Oriental and African Studies, University of London, London W.C.1, England. Length of time for editorial reports on submissions varies, since mss. are normally sent to an authority in the field for comments and criticisms.

JOURNAL OF ASIAN AND AFRICAN STUDIES

Editor: K. Ishwaran

Editorial address:
Department of Sociology
York University
Downsview, Ontario M3J 1P3, Canada

Frequency: Q   Founded: 1966
Subscription: $16.00

Editorial interest:
Chronological: unrestricted
Geographical: Africa, Asia
Topical: anthropology, foreign relations, international organizations,
research methods, social history, sociology

Editorial policies:
Style manual: none prescribed
Preferred length of ms.: 25 typed pages of 350 words per sheet; no
serialization
Author payment: one copy of issue in which article appears and 25
article reprints
Bottom notes. Accepts mss. and publishes articles in English. Wants mss.
in anthropology, history, sociology, and related social sciences.

Notes: Indexed in SSHI
Special feature: "Research Communications." Footnotes should be
numbered in Arabic numerals, starting anew on each page. Footnotes and bibliography should be kept as short as possible. It is
assumed that mss. submitted are in final form and will require
no further alterations. Authors will be charged for corrections
other than printer's errors. Freelance offerings of book reviews
are welcome; no remuneration.

JOURNAL OF BLACK STUDIES

Editor: Arthur L. Smith

Editorial address:
Sage Publications
275 South Beverly Drive
Beverly Hills, California 90212

Frequency: Q   Founded: 1970
Subscription: $10 individual; $8 student,   Subscribers: approximately
$15 institutional   1,000

Editorial interest:
Chronological: unrestricted
Geographical: Africa, Latin America, United States, West Indies
Topical: unrestricted
Special scope: analytical discussions of issues related to persons of
African descent

JOURNAL OF BLACK STUDIES (cont'd)

Editorial policies:

> Query letter prior to submission of ms. optional
>
> Style manual: "Notice to contributors to Sage Publications journals" available on request
>
> Preferred length of ms.: 25 typed pages maximum; longer articles for serialization occasionally considered
>
> Author payment: two copies of issue in which article appears and 24 article reprints
>
> End notes. Accepts mss. and publishes articles in English. Address mss. to Arthur L. Smith, Director, Afro-American Studies Center, University of California, Los Angeles, California 90024. Wants original, scholarly mss. on a broad range of questions involving Black people. Innovation encouraged, but the editor will favor mss. that demonstrate rigorous and thorough research in an inter-disciplinary context.

Notes:

> Special features: review essays. Potential authors should send two, or preferably three copies of ms.; identification (author's name and institution) should appear only on the title page. Book reviews are assigned, but freelance offerings are considered; no remuneration. Persons interested in reviewing should contact Ronald V. Downing, the book review editor, at the editorial address. Editorial reports on submissions within one to two months.

JOURNAL OF BUSINESS AND SOCIAL STUDIES

Editor: O. Oloko

Editorial address:

> School of Social Studies
> University of Lagos
> Nigeria

Sponsor: Schools of Administration and Social Studies, University of Lagos

Frequency: SA — Founded: 1969
Subscription: $4

Editorial interest:

> Chronological: unrestricted
> Geographical: Africa
> Topical: business, economics, politics and government, sociology

Editorial policies:

> Query prior to submission of ms. optional
>
> Style manual: consult previous issues
>
> Preferred length of ms.: 30 typed pages; no serialization to date but might be considered
>
> Author payment: five copies of issue in which article appears
>
> End notes. Accepts mss. and publishes articles in English. Mss. from abroad are welcomed.

JOURNAL OF BUSINESS AND SOCIAL STUDIES (cont'd)

Notes: Potential contributors should submit the original and two copies of the ms. All tables and illustrations are to be mounted on separate sheets. Freelance book reviews dealing with Africa and developing nations are welcomed; no remuneration. Persons interested in reviewing should contact the editor. Editorial reports on submissions as soon as possible.

JOURNAL OF COMMONWEALTH AND COMPARATIVE POLITICS

Editors: W. H. Morris-Jones and Colin Leys

Editorial address:
    Institute of Commonwealth Studies
    27 Russell Square
    London WC1B 5DS, England

Sponsor: Leicester University Press

Frequency: TA
Subscription: $15

Founded: 1961 (as *Journal of Commonwealth Political Studies*; name changed in 1974).

Editorial interest:
    Chronological: 1900 to present, current events
    Geographical: Africa, Asia, Canada, Pacific Area, West Indies
    Topical: foreign relations, international organizations, politics and
        government
    Special scope: Commonwealth affairs

Editorial policies:
    Query prior to submission of ms.
    Style manual: "A Note on Style" is available on request
    Preferred length of ms.: around 7,000 words; occasionally accepts longer
        articles for serialization
    Author payment: 25 article reprints
    End notes. Accepts mss. and publishes articles in English. Address mss.
        to Prof. W. H. Morris-Jones.

Notes: Articles abstracted in HA. Freelance book review offerings are not usually accepted.

JOURNAL OF COMMONWEALTH LITERATURE

Editor: Arthur Ravenscroft

Editorial address:
    School of English
    University of Leeds
    Leeds LS2 9JT, England

Sponsor: same as above

JOURNAL OF COMMONWEALTH LITERATURE (cont'd)

Frequency: SA

Founded: 1965

Subscription: £3.50/$9.50

Subscribers: approximately
1,200

Editorial interest:
>   Chronological: unrestricted (mostly twentieth century)
>   Geographical: Africa, Asia, Australia, Canada, West Indies
>   Topical: bibliographical articles, folklore, frontier areas, literature
>   (history and criticism), theatre and drama
>   Special scope: member states of the former British Commonwealth,
>   except Britain

Editorial policies:
>   Query prior to submission of ms. optional
>   Style manual: Oxford University Press
>   Preferred length of ms.: 3,000-5,000 words; no serialization
>   Author payment: £4 per 1,000 words
>   End notes. Accepts mss. and publishes articles in English. Potential
>   authors should write for an audience interested in English litera-
>   ture or in English and other languages in such countries (e.g.,
>   Canada, India) where literatures are influenced by English and other
>   languages. Audience consists chiefly of literary scholars and stu-
>   dents, but there is also a general audience likely to be interested in
>   the art of letters. Wants shorter rather than longer mss., critical or
>   historical, but written concisely, clearly, and with a sense of style.

Notes: Articles abstracted in AES
>   Special feature: December issue contains "Annual Bibliography of
>   Commonwealth Literature" for the previous year. Potential authors
>   should submit original and one copy of ms., typed, double-spaced;
>   titles of published volumes in italics, titles of parts of volumes in
>   single quotation marks; quoted passages in single-spaced typing, but
>   not indented. Book reviews are normally assigned, but freelance
>   reviews will be seriously considered; remuneration £3 per 1,000
>   words. Preferable length of review: 900 words or in multiples of
>   450 words, allowing 50-60 words for heading and signature.
>   Persons interested in reviewing should contact the editor.

JOURNAL OF DEVELOPING AREAS

Editor: Spencer H. Brown

Editorial address:
>   Western Illinois University
>   Macomb, Illinois 61455

Sponsor: same as above

Frequency: Q

Founded: 1966

Subscription: $9 individual; $12 institution;
    $7 outside North America

Subscribers: 1,600

JOURNAL OF DEVELOPING AREAS (cont'd)

Editorial interest:

    Chronological: unrestricted

    Geographical: worldwide

    Topical: agriculture, architecture, art, auxiliary historical disciplines, bibliographical articles, business, church or ecclesiastical affairs, communications media, cultural affairs, economics, education, foreign relations, frontier areas, geography, legal and constitutional affairs, literature (history and criticism), medicine (history), military affairs, politics and government, research methods, science and technology, social history, sociology, transportation

    Special scope: interdisciplinary, descriptive, theoretical, and comparative study of regional development in order to understand man's relationship to the developmental process

Editorial policies:

    Style manual: Chicago; potential contributors should request sheets on editorial principles and ms. preparation

    Preferred length of ms.: 20-30 typed pages; longer articles for serialization are accepted

    Author payment: two copies of issue in which article appears and 50 article reprints

    End notes. Articles published in English or French. Encourages articles on development from all fields in the humanities and social sciences. Mss. should be addressed to the general editor.

Notes: Articles abstracted or indexed in AHL, APS, *Book Review Index for Social Science Periodicals*, CC, *Economic Abstracts*, *GEO Abstracts*, HA.

    Special features: a bibliographic section of current periodical literature and monographs, and a news and notes section that gives information on study programs, fellowship opportunities, and research projects. Book reviews are assigned. Persons interested in reviewing may submit name, qualifications, and areas of specialty to book review editor; no remuneration. Reports on submissions in two to four months.

JOURNAL OF DEVELOPMENT STUDIES: A Quarterly Journal Devoted to Economic, Political and Social Development

Managing editors: David Lehman and Michael Lipton

Editorial address:

    Frank Cass and Company Ltd.

    67 Great Russell Street

    London WC 1B 3BT, England

Frequency: Q   Founded: 1964

Subscription: £7/$21   Subscribers: 1,500

JOURNAL OF DEVELOPMENT STUDIES (cont'd)

Editorial interest:
    Chronological: unrestricted
    Geographical: worldwide
    Topical: economics, international organizations, politics and government, sociology

Editorial policies:
    Potential contributors should request this journal's style sheet before submitting a completed ms.
    Preferred length of ms.: 5,000-10,000 words; no serialization
    Author payment: 25 article reprints
    Address mss. to The Secretary. Authors must address themselves to an international audience with very high professional standards. Wants articles that raise issues of broad significance.

Notes: Articles abstracted or indexed in APS, JEL.

JOURNAL OF ETHIOPIAN LAW

Editorial address:
    Faculty of Law
    Haile Selassie I University
    Box 1176
    Addis Ababa, Ethiopia

Sponsor: same as above

Frequency: SA   Founded: 1964
Subscription: $18 patrons; $7 (plus   Subscribers: 200
    postage) individual

Editorial interest:
    Chronological: unrestricted
    Geographical: Ethiopia
    Topical: international law, legal and constitutional affairs
    Special scope: Ethiopian development, especially legal development

Editorial policies:
    Style manual: none prescribed, mss. edited by staff
    Preferred length of ms.: 30 typed pages; no serialization
    Author payment: 10 article reprints
    End notes. Accepts mss. and publishes articles in Amharic or English. Potential authors should write for an audience of comparative lawyers. Wants mss. on Ethiopian law.

Notes: Freelance book reviews welcomed; no remuneration. Editorial decisions on submissions within five months.

JOURNAL OF ETHIOPIAN STUDIES

Editors: Richard Pankhurst, S. Chojnacki, and Hazel Relton

Editorial address:
Institute of Ethiopian Studies
Haile Selassie I University
P.O. Box 1896
Addis Ababa, Ethiopia

Sponsor: same as above

Frequency: SA   Founded: 1963
Subscription: $30   Subscribers: 1,000

Editorial interest:
Chronological: unrestricted
Geographical: Ethiopia
Topical: anthropology, archaeology, architecture, art, auxiliary historical disciplines, bibliographical articles, church or ecclesiastical
affairs, cultural affairs, demography, discovery and exploration,
economics, education, ethnology, folklore, foreign relations,
frontier areas, geography, historiography, history of ideas,
language (philology, semantics), literature (history and criticism),
medicine (history), military affairs, music (history), philosophy,
politics and government, religious studies, sociology

Editorial policies:
Query prior to submission of ms. optional
Style manual: own house style, contact editor
Preferred length of ms.: any; no serialization
Author payment: 30 article reprints
Bottom or end notes. Accepts mss. and publishes articles in Amharic,
English, French, German, or Italian. Potential authors should
write for a scholarly audience interested in Ethiopian affairs.

Notes: Articles cited in *Africa*. No book reviews.

JOURNAL OF MODERN AFRICAN STUDIES

Editor: David Kimble

Editorial address:
Cambridge University Press
32 East 57th Street
New York, New York 10022

Frequency: Q   Founded: 1963
Subscription: £5.50/$15 individual;   Subscribers: 3,826
£7.50/$23.50 institutional

Editorial interest:
Chronological: unrestricted
Geographical: Africa

JOURNAL OF MODERN AFRICAN STUDIES (cont'd)

Topical: economics, education, international law, politics and government, science and technology, social history, sociology
Special scope: current and future literature and literary trends

Editorial policies:
Query prior to submission of ms. optional
Style manual: refer to previous issues
Preferred length of ms.: 3,000-6,000 words and occasionally up to
10,000; longer articles for serialization occasionally accepted
Author payment: 25 article reprints
Bottom notes. Accepts mss. in any modern language. Publishes articles
in English. Queries and mss. should be addressed to the editor at
the University of Botswana, Lesotho, and Swaziland; P.O. Roma;
Maseru, Lesotho, Southern Africa. Potential authors should write
for a scholarly audience of Africanists.

Notes: Articles abstracted in HA
Special feature: "Africana." Book reviews are assigned and solicited, but
freelance offerings are considered. Persons interested in reviewing
should contact the editor. Editorial reports on submissions in six
weeks.

JOURNAL OF NEGRO EDUCATION

Editor: Charles A. Martin

Associate editor: Theresa A. Rector

Editorial address:
Howard University
Washington, D.C. 20001

Sponsor: same as above

Frequency: Q
Subscription: $5

Founded: 1931
Subscribers: 3,000

Editorial interest:
Chronological: unrestricted
Geographical: Africa, United States (mostly), (occasional articles with
international scope)
Topical: education

Editorial policies:
Style manual: Chicago
Preferred length of ms.: 10-25 typed pages
Author payment: three copies of issue concerned
End notes. Would like to see stimulating opinion or position articles.
Articles must be related in some way to the education of Black
Americans (historical, philosophical, sociological, psychological,
etc.).

JOURNAL OF NEGRO EDUCATION (cont'd)

Notes: Articles abstracted or indexed in *Book Review Index*, EI, PA, SA.
Book reviews are assigned, but will also accept freelance; no remuneration. Reports on submissions in eight weeks.

JOURNAL OF NEGRO HISTORY

Editor: W. Augustus Low

Editorial address:
P.O. Box 7694
Baltimore, Maryland 21207

Sponsor: Association for the Study of Negro Life and History

Frequency: Q
Subscription: $10 U.S.; $10.50 elsewhere

Founded: 1916
Subscribers: 6,000

Editorial interest:
Chronological: unrestricted
Geographical: worldwide
Topical: anthropology, art, bibliographical articles, discovery and exploration, education, historiography, history of ideas, international organizations, maritime history, medicine (history), music (history), social history

Editorial policies:
Query prior to submission of ms.
Style manual: unspecified
Preferred length of ms.: 20 typed pages; accepts longer articles for serialization
Author payment: five copies of issue in which article appears
End notes: Welcomes scholarly articles and historical mss. relating to the Black people around the world. Encourages study of new aspects of Negro life.

Notes: Articles abstracted or indexed in AHL, HA, SSHI. Book reviews are assigned, but occasionally accepts freelance offerings; no remuneration.

JOURNAL OF RELIGION IN AFRICA

Editor: A. F. Walls

Editorial address:
Department of Religious Studies
University of Aberdeen
Aberdeen, Scotland

Frequency: TA
Subscription: Dfl 48

Founded: 1967
Subscribers: 508

Editorial interest:
Chronological: unrestricted
Geographical: Africa

JOURNAL OF RELIGION IN AFRICA (cont'd)

Topical: church or ecclesiastical affairs, religious studies

Editorial policies:
>Style manual: none prescribed
>Preferred length of ms.: 10-25 typed pages; no serialization
>Author payment: 25 article reprints, 10 reprints of short notes
>End notes. Accepts mss. and publishes articles in English or French

Notes: Book reviews are assigned; no remuneration. Editorial reports on submissions in a few weeks.

JOURNAL OF SEMITIC STUDIES

Editors: James Barr and C. E. Bosworth

Editorial address:
>Manchester University
>Manchester M13 9PL, England

Sponsor: same as above

Frequency: SA   Founded: 1956
Subscription: £5

Editorial interest:
>Chronological: unrestricted
>Geographical: Africa, Middle East
>Topical: anthropology, archaeology, language (linguistics, philology, semantics), literature (history and criticism), philosophy
>Special scope: Accadian, Arabic, and Jewish studies

Editorial policies:
>Query letter prior to submission of ms. optional
>Style manual: none
>Preferred length of ms.: unspecified
>Author payment: 25 article reprints
>Bottom notes. Accepts mss. and publishes articles in English, French, or German. Wants mss. on linguistics, philology, and semantics.

Notes: Articles abstracted in HA. Book reviews are assigned, but freelance offerings are considered; no remuneration.

JOURNAL OF THE NEW AFRICAN LITERATURE AND THE ARTS

Editor: Joseph Okpaku

Assistant editor: Ode Okore

Editorial address:
>444 Central Park West
>New York, New York 10025

Sponsor: The Third Press

JOURNAL OF THE NEW AFRICAN LITERATURE AND THE ARTS (cont'd)

Frequency: Q

Founded: 1966

Subscription: $10

Subscribers: 1,500

Editorial interest:
> Chronological: unrestricted
> Geographical: Africa, United States, West Indies
> Topical: anthropology, archaeology, art, auxiliary historical disciplines, communications media, cultural affairs, education, folklore, language (philology, semantics), literature (history and criticism), music (history), theatre and drama

Editorial policies:
> Style manual: any
> Preferred length of ms.: 1-20 typed pages; accepts longer articles for serialization
> Author payment: none except when articles are included in an anthology
> End notes. Accepts mss. and publishes articles in English or French. Wants mss. on literary criticism.

Notes: Book reviews are solicited and assigned; no remuneration.

JOURNAL OF THE S.W.A. SCIENTIFIC SOCIETY

Editor: H. J. Rust

Editorial address:
> S.W.A. Scientific Society
> P.O. Box 67
> Windhoek, South West Africa

Sponsor: South West African Scientific Society

Frequency: A

Founded: 1925

Subscription: Rds 4 (includes *Newsletter*)

Subscribers: approximately 650

Editorial interest:
> Chronological: unrestricted
> Geographical: Africa
> Topical: anthropology, archaeology, bibliographical articles, ethnology, geography, literature (history and criticism)
> Special scope: South West Africa

Editorial policies:
> Query prior to submission of ms.
> Style manual: none prescribed
> Preferred length of ms.: any; serialization accepted
> Author payment: 50 article reprints
> Bottom notes. Accepts mss. and publishes articles in Afrikaans, English, or German. Wants mss. of a scientific nature.

JOURNAL OF THE S.W.A. SCIENTIFIC SOCIETY (cont'd)

Notes: Indexed in CC
> Special features: South West African science. The Society also publishes a monograph series relating to South West Africa. Book reviews are solicited. Persons interested in reviewing should contact the editor; no remuneration. Editorial decisions on submissions vary with the length of the mss.; normally a report can be expected within one month. Illustrated.

JOURNAL OF TROPICAL GEOGRAPHY

Editor: Ooi Jin Bee

Associate editor: Warwick Neville

Editorial address:
> Department of Geography
> University of Singapore
> Singapore 10

Sponsors: University of Singapore and University of Malaya

Frequency: SA   Founded: 1953
Subscription: $10   Subscribers: 900

Editorial interest:
> Chronological: unrestricted
> Geographical: Africa, Asia, Latin America (all tropical areas)
> Topical: agriculture, anthropology, discovery and exploration, economics, geography, sociology, transportation

Editorial policies:
> Style manual: instructions on back cover of journal
> Preferred length of ms.: 4,000-6,000 words; occasionally accepts longer articles for serialization
> Author payment: 25 article reprints
> Bottom notes

Notes: Articles abstracted in *Biological Abstracts*

KLEIO: Bulletin of the Department of History, University of South Africa

Editor: A. L. Harrington

Editorial address:
> Department of History
> University of South Africa
> P.O. Box 392
> Pretoria, South Africa

Sponsor: Publications Committee, University of South Africa

KLEIO (cont'd)

Frequency: SA   Founded: 1969
Subscription: distributed free to students
     of the University of South Africa
     and to interested institutions

Editorial interest:
     Chronological: unrestricted
     Geographical: worldwide
     Topical: anthropology, archaeology, architecture, auxiliary historical
          disciplines, bibliographical articles, church or ecclesiastical affairs,
          discovery and exploration, economics, education, foreign rela-
          tions, frontier areas, geography, historiography, history of ideas,
          maritime history, military affairs, naval affairs, philosophy of
          history, politics and government, research methods, social history,
          transportation

Editorial policies:
     Query prior to submission of ms.
     Style manual: *Hart's Rules for Compositors and Readers* (Oxford
          University Press)
     Preferred length of ms.: approximately 4,000 words; will accept
          articles of merit for serialization
     Author payment: three copies of issue in which article appears
     End notes. Accepts and publishes mss. in Afrikaans, Dutch, or English.
          Authors should direct articles toward scholarly, academic audience.
          Journal focus is primarily as a teaching medium, secondly as a
          vehicle for the publication of new material concerning Africa.

Notes: Articles cited and indexed in HA, *Select Bibliography of South Afri-
     can History*
     Special features: indexed listing of articles appearing in recent journals
          relevant to specific topical areas. Book reviews assigned; no remun-
          eration. Editorial reports on submissions in three weeks.

KRONIEK VAN AFRIKA

Editors: A. E. Bayer, P. A. Emanuel, K. L. Roskam

Editorial address:
     Stationsplein 10
     Leyden, The Netherlands

Sponsor: Afrika-Studiecentrum

Frequency: Q   Founded: 1961
Subscription: Dfl 21   Subscribers: 500

Editorial interest:
     Chronological: 1600 to present, current events
     Geographical: Africa

KRONIEK VAN AFRIKA (cont'd)

Topical: anthropology, bibliographical articles, cultural affairs, demography, economics, education, international organizations, legal and constitutional affairs, literature (history and criticism), politics and government, sociology

Special scope: customary law

Editorial policies:

Query prior to submission of ms.

Style manual: none prescribed

Preferred length of ms.: 15-20 typed pages; rarely considers longer articles for serialization

Author payment: Dfl 100 and 25 article reprints

End notes. Accepts mss. and publishes articles in Dutch, English, French, or German. Potential authors should write for an academic audience interested in current African affairs. ✹

Notes: Articles cited in *Bulletin Analytique*

Special features: for Dutch readers, editorial features on current events in selected African countries, documents. Book reviews are assigned and solicited; persons interested in reviewing should contact the editors; no remuneration. Editorial reports on submissions in two weeks.

LEGON OBSERVER

Editor: P.A.V. Ansah

Editorial address:
P.O. Box 11
Legon, Ghana

Sponsor: Legon Society on National Affairs

Frequency: BW

Subscription: $11.75 surface; $27.30 airmail

Founded: 1966

Subscribers: approximately 8,000

Editorial interest:

Chronological: current events

Geographical: Africa

Topical: agriculture, cultural affairs, economics, education, foreign relations, politics and government, sociology

Special scope: emphasis on Africa but also interested in articles showing how outsiders view Africa and its problems

Editorial policies:

Style manual: none prescribed

Preferred length of ms.: 5-10 typed pages, quarto size. Occasionally accepts longer articles for serialization.

Author payment: $15 for commissioned articles, four copies of issue in which article appears for unsolicited articles

LEGON OBSERVER (cont'd)

Discourages reference notes; when they are necessary they should be end notes. Accepts mss. and publishes articles in English. Potential authors should write for an audience of a wide range of people; not interested in abstract theories.

Notes: Articles cited in SSHI
Special feature: a letters column which gives cross-section of opinion on matters of current interest in Ghana. Book reviews are generally assigned or solicited, but freelance offerings considered. Reports on submissions in two weeks.

LIBERIAN STUDIES JOURNAL

Editors: Svend E. Holsoe and David M. Foley

Editorial address:
Department of Anthropology
University of Delaware
Newark, Delaware 19711

Sponsor: Liberian Studies Association in America

Frequency: SA   Founded: 1968
Subscription: $6 individual; $7 institutional   Subscribers: 250

Editorial interest:
Chronological: unrestricted
Geographical: Liberia
Topical: unrestricted

Editorial policies:
Query prior to submission of ms.
Style manual: Kate L. Turabian, *A Manual for Writers*
Preferred length of ms.: none; accepts articles for serialization
Author payment: 15 article reprints
Bottom notes. Accepts mss. and publishes articles in English. Address mss. to Svend E. Holsoe.

Notes: Articles abstracted or cited by African Bibliography Center, International African Institute. Mss. should be double-spaced if pica type, and triple-spaced if elite type. Book reviews are assigned and solicited, but freelance offerings are considered; no remuneration.

LITERATURE EAST AND WEST

Editor: Roy E. Teele

Book editor: William Schultz

Editorial address:
Box 8107
University Station
Austin, Texas 78912

LITERATURE EAST AND WEST (cont'd)

Sponsor: Comparative Literature 9, MLA

Frequency: Q
Subscription: $8

Founded: 1954
Subscribers: 6,500

Editorial interest:
> Chronological: unrestricted
> Geographical: Africa, Asia, Middle East, Pacific Area
> Topical: literature (history and criticism), theatre and drama
> Special scope: translations of poetry, drama, and fiction

Editorial policies:
> Style manual: Chicago
> Preferred length of ms.: 15-20 typed pages; longer articles rarely
> accepted for serialization
> Author payment: 25 article reprints
> End notes. Accepts and publishes mss. in English, or occasionally French.
> Potential authors should write for a literary college readership,
> but meet the demands of scholar-peers. Would like to see trans-
> lations of poetry, drama, and fiction, literary criticism (historical
> or "explicative"), and comparative literary criticism.

Notes: Articles indexed and abstracted in HA, MLA
> Special features: issues devoted to a national literature. Book reviews are
> usually assigned; no remuneration except for books and reprints.
> Write to William Schultz, Chairman Oriental Studies, University of
> Arizona, Tucson, Arizona. Reports on submissions in two weeks
> to six months.

LOTUS: Magazine of Afro-Asian Writings

Editor: Youssef El Sebai

Editorial address:
> 104 Kasr el Aini Street
> Cairo, United Arab Republic

Sponsor: Afro-Asian Writers Association

Frequency: Q
Subscription: $8

Founded: 1968
Subscribers: 200

Editorial interest:
> Chronological: 1900 to present
> Geographical: Africa, Asia, Eastern Europe, Latin America, Middle
> East, Russia/USSR
> Topical: anthropology, architecture, art, cultural affairs, education,
> ethnology, folklore, history of ideas, language (philology,
> semantics), literature (history and criticism), music (history),
> philosophy, philosophy of history, politics and government,
> religious studies, social history, sociology, theatre and drama
> Special scope: Afro-Asian literatures and arts

LOTUS (cont'd)

Editorial policies:
> Query prior to submission of ms.
> Style manual: none prescribed
> Preferred length of ms.: 10-15 typed pages; no serialization
> Author payment: cash honorarium
> End notes. Accepts Arabic, English, French, Portuguese, and Spanish
> > language mss. Articles published in Arabic, English, or French.

Notes:
> Special features: documents on the Afro-Asian writers' movement.
> > Accepts freelance book reviews; slight remuneration. Persons
> > interested in book reviewing are invited to write to the editor.
> > Reports on queries and submissions in three months.

MANKIND QUARTERLY

Editor: R. Gayre of Gayre

Assistant editors: Robert Kuttner and Robert H. S. Robertson

Editorial address:
> 1 Darnaway Street
> Edinburgh EH3 6DW, Scotland

Frequency: Q   Founded: 1960
Subscription: $5.50/£1.50; $15.40/£4 for
> 3 years; $5.50/£1.50 per year extra
> for air mail

Editorial interest:
> Chronological: unrestricted
> Geographical: worldwide
> Topical: demography, ethnology, geography
> Special scope: "an international quarterly journal dealing with race and
> > inheritance in the fields of ethnology, ethno- and human genetics,
> > ethno-psychology, racial history, demography and anthropo-
> > geography"

Editorial policies:
> Preferred length of ms.: 15-30 typed pages
> Author payment: $2.50 per printed page and 12 copies of issue
> > concerned
> Bottom notes. *Mankind Quarterly* "fulfils the need for a conservative
> > and scientific approach to the human sciences."

Notes: Contains numerous short book reviews; most, however, are staff
> written. Editors prefer mss. in triplicate. Mss. may be accompanied by a
> short biographical note and suitable photograph for inclusion if space
> permits.

MANPOWER AND UNEMPLOYMENT RESEARCH IN AFRICA: A Newsletter

Editors: Peter C. W. Gutkind, Peter Carstens, and André Lux

Editorial address:
> 3437 Peel Street
> Centre for Developing Area Studies
> McGill University
> Montreal 112, P. Quebec, Canada

Sponsor: same as above

Frequency: SA   Founded: 1968
Subscription: $2.50   Subscribers: 517

Editorial interest:
> Chronological: unrestricted, current events (mainly)
> Geographical: Africa (mainly), Asia, Latin America, Pacific Area, West Indies
> Topical: agriculture, anthropology, business, economics, education, geography, management, politics and government, research methods, science and technology, sociology, transportation
> Special scope: unemployment problems

Editorial policies:
> Preferred length of ms.: 4-30 typed pages; longer articles accepted for serialization
> Author payment: approximately five article reprints
> End notes. Accepts and publishes mss. in English or French

Notes:
> Special feature: bibliography at back of most issues compiled by Peter C. W. Gutkind. Accepts freelance book reviews; no remuneration. Send to Peter C. W. Gutkind. Reports on submissions in three weeks.

MILITARY HISTORY JOURNAL

Editor-in-chief: G. R. Duxbury

Honorary editor: D. P. Tidy

Editorial address:
> P.O. Box 52090
> Saxonwold, Transvaal, South Africa

Sponsor: South African National War Museum

Frequency: SA   Founded: 1967
Subscription: Rds 2.50 in the Republic   Subscribers: 400
> of South Africa, Rds 3 elsewhere

Editorial interest:
> Chronological: unrestricted (mainly eighteenth and nineteenth centuries)
> Geographical: worldwide (mainly South Africa)

Topical: air forces, military affairs, naval affairs
Special scope: all aspects of military history

Editorial policies:
Query prior to submission of ms.
Style manual: none prescribed
Preferred length of ms.: 3,000-5,000 words; accepts longer articles
for serialization
Author payment: one copy of issue in which article appears
End notes. Accepts mss. and publishes articles in Afrikaans or English

Notes: Prefers book reviews of technical works directly relating to South
African military history or South African military forces. Persons
interested in reviewing should contact the editor-in-chief.

MUNGER AFRICANA LIBRARY NOTES

Editors: Robert Bates, Margaret R. Bates, Robert Dilworth, Robert
Huttenback, Edwin Munger, Robert Oliver, and Thayer Scudder

Assistant editors: Monique Le Blanc and Joanne Clark

Editorial address:
Munger Africana Library
California Institute of Technology
Pasadena, California 91109

Sponsor: same as above

Frequency: BM   Founded: 1970
Subscription: $10

Editorial interest:
Chronological: unrestricted
Geographical: Africa
Topical: unrestricted

Editorial policies:
Query prior to submission of ms.
Style manual: Chicago
Preferred length of ms.: 30-150 typed pages; no serialization
Bottom or end notes. "Topics are eclectic within the field of Africana."
Issues are generated from seminars, reports of current research,
unpublished historical mss., and other material deemed useful to
Africanists. Illustrated with maps and colored photos.

Notes: Monograph series. No book reviews.

LE MUSEON: Revue d'Etudes Orientales

Editors: P. Vandenven, R. Draguet, J. Ries, and G. Garitte

Editorial address:
G. Garitte
9 Beukenlaan
3030 Heverlee, Belgium

Sponsor: Association "Le Muséon"

Frequency: 2 double volumes per year   Founded: 1881
Subscription: 750 BeFr (postage not
included)

Editorial interest:
Chronological: 410 to 1492
Geographical: Africa, Asia, Mediterranean, Middle East
Topical: anthropology, archaeology, auxiliary historical disciplines,
bibliographical articles, church or ecclesiastical affairs, historiography, history of ideas, language (philology, semantics), literature
(history and criticism), philosophy, religious studies

Editorial policies:
Query prior to submission of ms.
Preferred length of ms.: 20-40 typed pages; longer articles accepted for
serialization
Author payment: BeFr 30 per page, and 50 complimentary article
reprints
End notes. Accepts and publishes mss. in French, English, German, or
Italian.

Notes: Freelance book reviews accepted; no remuneration. Reports on submissions in two to three weeks. Illustrated.

**MUSLIM WORLD: A Journal Devoted to the Study of Islam and of the
Christian-Muslim Relationship in the Past and the Present**

Editor: Willem A. Bijlefeld

Co-editor: Issa J. Boullata

Editorial address:
Hartford Seminary Foundation
55 Elizabeth Street
Hartford, Connecticut 06105

Sponsor: same as above

Frequency: Q   Founded: 1911
Subscription: $6   Subscribers: approximately
1,200

Editorial interest:
Chronological: pre-Islamic Arabia to the present Muslim world
Geographical: Africa, Asia, Middle East, Pacific Area, USSR (Muslim
areas)

MUSLIM WORLD (cont'd)

Topical: church or ecclesiastical affairs, history of ideas, language (philology, semantics), legal and constitutional affairs, literature (history and criticism), philosophy, social history, sociology
Special scope: Islamic studies, Christian-Muslim relations

Editorial policies:
Query prior to submission of ms.
Style manual: Kate L. Turabian, *A Manual for Writers*; for transliteration of Arabic, use the *Encyclopedia of Islam*
Preferred length of ms.: average 6,600 words to a maximum of 9,300 words; occasionally accepts longer articles for serialization
Author payment: 20 article reprints or five copies of issue in which article appears
End notes. Accepts mss. and publishes articles in English but a few words or lines of Arabic, Urdu, Persian can be included. Potential authors should write for an audience of teachers, research scholars, students, missionaries and others interested in Muslim-Christian relations and intercultural concerns. Wants scholarly studies of Islam and Muslim-Christian relations.

Notes: Articles abstracted or indexed in HA, *Journal of Ecumenical Studies*, *Liste mondiale des périodiques spécialisés en sciences sociales*, *Middle East and North Africa*, *Religious Periodicals Index*.
Special features: "Notes on the Quarter," "Survey of Periodicals." Potential contributors should double-space everything including indented quotations and reference notes. Hyphens at end of lines should be avoided and American rules for spelling and punctuation should be followed. Book reviews are solicited; freelance offerings of around 850 words are sometimes accepted, but query letter must be submitted. Persons interested in reviewing should contact the book review editor at the editorial address. Editorial reports on submissions as soon as possible; no fixed time on unsolicited mss.

NADA: The Rhodesia Government Ministry of Internal Affairs Annual

Editor: J. L. Fubbs

Editorial address:
Private Bag 7702
Causeway, Salisbury, Rhodesia

Sponsor: Rhodesia Government Ministry of Internal Affairs (this is not a government publication)

Frequency: A
Subscription: unreported

Founded: 1923
Subscribers: 2,500

Editorial interest:
Chronological: unrestricted
Geographical: Central and Southern Africa

NADA (cont'd)

    Topical: anthropology, archaeology, art, bibliographical articles, cultural affairs, discovery and exploration, education, folklore, music (history), philosophy, sociology

    Special scope: customs, legends, traditions

Editorial policies:

    Style manual: none prescribed

    Preferred length of ms.: 10-25 typed pages; accepts longer articles for serialization

    Author payment: one copy of issue in which article appears

    End notes, but reference notes are discouraged. Accepts mss. in all modern African and West European languages, publishes articles in English. Wants articles that will bring about a greater understanding of the African people, but the articles must be factual. Does not publish fiction or political opinions of any sort. Welcomes mss. on African customs and Rhodesian history.

Notes: Abstracted in HA. Book reviews are staff-written. Illustrated in color.

NATIONAL SCENE MAGAZINE SUPPLEMENT

Editor: L. H. Stanton

Editorial address:
    507 5th Avenue
    New York, New York 10017

Sponsor: L. H. Stanton Publications, Inc.

Frequency: M
Subscription: varies

Founded: 1947
Subscribers: 78 Black-owned weekly newspapers

Editorial interest:

    Chronological: 1600 to present

    Geographical: Africa, Latin America, United States, West Indies

    Topical: bibliographical articles, business, church or ecclesiastical affairs, cinema and film, communications media, cultural affairs, economics, education, ethnology, folklore, frontier areas, geography, legal and constitutional affairs, literature (history and criticism), medicine (history), military affairs, naval affairs, philosophy, politics and government, religious studies, science and technology, social history, theatre and drama

    Special scope: Black interests

Editorial policies:

    Style manual: none prescribed; see previous issues

    Preferred length of ms.: 2,000 words; longer articles for serialization accepted

    Author payment: cash payment varies, article reprints as requested

    End notes.

Notes: Book reviews are assigned, but freelance offerings are considered; no remuneration. Reports on submissions as soon as possible.

NEGRO AMERICAN LITERATURE FORUM

Editor: Hannah Hedrick

Editorial address:
> School of Education
> Indiana State University
> Terre Haute, Indiana 47809

Sponsor: same as above

Frequency: Q   Founded: 1966
Subscription: $4

Editorial interest:
> Chronological: current events
> Geographical: Africa, United States (mostly)
> Topical: art, bibliographical articles, cultural affairs, literature, politics and government, theatre and drama
> Special scope: Black American autobiography, fiction and poetry

Editorial policies:
> Query prior to submission of ms.
> Style manual: none specified
> Preferred length of ms.: 1,500-4,000 words
> End notes. Potential authors should write for school and university teachers.

Notes:
> Special features: review articles of Black American literature written by leading scholars. No book reviews. Illustrated.

NEGRO EDUCATIONAL REVIEW: A Forum for Discussion of Afro-American Issues

Editor-in-chief: J. Irving E. Scott

Managing editor: R. Grann Lloyd

Editorial address:
> P.O. Box 2895
> West Bay Annes
> Jacksonville, Florida 32203

Frequency: Q   Founded: 1949
Subscription: $7.50

Editorial interest:
> Chronological: current events
> Geographical: Africa, United States

NEGRO EDUCATIONAL REVIEW (cont'd)

> Topical: business, economics, education, language, literature, research methods, sociology

Editorial policies:
> Query prior to submission of ms.
> Style manual: Chicago
> Preferred length of ms.: 5,000-8,000 words
> Address mss. to managing editor. "The *Negro Educational Review* seeks to present scholarly articles and research reports, competent analysis and descriptions of current problems and significant compilations."

Notes: Book reviews are assigned, but freelance offerings from well-established scholars are considered. Persons interested in reviewing should contact the book review editor, Hortense D. Lloyd, at the editorial address.

NEGRO HISTORY BULLETIN

Editor: J. Rupert Picott

Editorial address:
> 1407 14th Street, N.W.
> Washington, D.C. 20005

Sponsor: Association for the Study of Negro Life and History

Frequency: 8 xy.   Founded: 1937
Subscription: $6   Subscribers: 22,000

Editorial interest:
> Chronological: unrestricted
> Geographical: worldwide
> Topical: unrestricted
> Special scope: field of Negro history and Black studies

Editorial policies:
> Preferred length of ms.: 4-10 typed pages; longer articles accepted for serialization if important enough
> Author payment: five complimentary article reprints
> End notes preferred. Would like to see articles involving Black people or persons who have related themselves to the field.

Notes: Articles indexed in *Index to Periodical Articles By and About Negroes* (G. K. Hall). Book reviews are usually solicited; no remuneration. They should be short and specific. Reports on submissions of some mss. may take as long as three to four months in order to fit them into a specific issue.

NEWSLETTER OF THE WESTERN ASSOCIATION OF AFRICANISTS

Editor: Robert M. Wren

Editorial address:
Office of International Affairs
University of Houston
Houston, Texas 77004

Sponsor: Western Association of Africanists

Frequency: TA
Subscription: $2 faculty and non-academic;
$1 student; $7.50 institutional

Founded: 1969
Circulation: 500

Editorial interest:
Chronological: unrestricted
Geographical: Africa
Topical: unrestricted
Special scope: business of the Western Association of Africanists; news
relevant to research and teaching about Africa in Western United
States

Editorial policies:
Preferred length of ms.: 100-600 words, but no policy is set. Does not at
present accept articles for serialization.
Author payment: none at present, but will supply article reprints as
requested
Footnotes should normally be avoided. Potential authors should write
for an audience composed of the members of the Western Association of Africanists. Their special interest is in finding means to
improve research and teaching competence in colleges and uni-
versities distant from major centers of African studies. Editor
notes: "the nature of the *Newsletter* has been changing continually,
and we expect to change as our situation warrants."

Notes:
Special features: news of conferences, speaker availabilities, significant
publications, fellowships and scholarships, study programs in the
United States and Africa, reports on activities of the Western
Association of Africanists. Unsolicited book reviews are accepted,
but are not being sought. Reviews are very brief at present. Reports
on submissions "promptly."

ODU—NEW SERIES: A Journal of West African Studies

Editor: Michael Crowder

Assistant editor: A. O. Anjorin

Editorial address:
Institute of African Studies
University of Ife
Ile-Ife, Nigeria

ODU—NEW SERIES (cont'd)

Sponsor: same as above

Frequency: SA
Subscription: N 25s in Nigeria; $4.75/£1.60
    elsewhere (including postage)

Founded: 1964-1968 (old
    series); 1969 (new
    series)
Subscribers: approximately
    750

Editorial interest:
    Chronological: unrestricted
    Geographical: West Africa
    Topical: unrestricted

Editorial policies:
    Query prior to submission of ms.
    Style manual: *Author's and Printer's Dictionary* (Oxford University
        Press); "Notes on Style" available on request
    Preferred length of ms.: 7,500-10,000 words; no serialization
    Author payment: 25 article reprints
    End notes. Accepts mss. and publishes articles in English. Address mss.
        to the editor. Potential authors should write for an audience
        interested in West African studies. Wants scholarly mss. on the
        entire spectrum of West African studies, with emphasis on inten-
        sive local research.

Notes: Articles abstracted in HA. Book reviews are assigned or solicited at the
editor's discretion; no remuneration. Editorial reports on submissions in
three months.

OKIKE: An African Journal of New Writing

Editor: Chinua Achebe

Editorial address:
    Nwamife Publishers
    10 Ibiam Street
    Enugu, ECS Nigeria

Frequency: TA
Subscription: $6/£2.50

Founded: 1971
Subscribers: 2,000

Editorial interest:
    Chronological: current events
    Geographical: worldwide (emphasis on Africa)
    Topical: literature (history and criticism)
    Special scope: poetry, short stories

Editorial policies:
    No author payment at present.

Notes:
    Special features: new original writing from Africa and elsewhere. Book
        reviews are assigned, but will accept freelance offerings; no remun-
        eration at present. Reports on submissions in two months.

ORITA: Ibadan Journal of Religious Studies

Editor: Muizz Goriawala

Editorial address:
Department of Religious Studies
University of Ibadan
Ibadan, Nigeria

Sponsor: same as above

Frequency: SA
Subscription: £3/$5.50

Founded: 1967
Subscribers: approximately
500

Editorial interest:
Chronological: unrestricted
Geographical: Africa
Topical: religious studies
Special scope: social implication and interaction of African traditional
religion, Christianity, and Islam

Editorial policies:
Style manual: consult previous issues
Preferred length of ms.: 4,000-5,000 words; serialization of longer
articles considered
Author payment: three copies of issue in which article appears
End notes. Accepts mss. and publishes articles in English. Wants mss. on
any of the three religions (African traditional, Christianity, or
Islam) with special reference to Africa.

Notes: Indexed in SSHI
Special feature: research notes. Book reviews are assigned and solicited.
Editorial reports on submissions in two to three months.

OVERSEAS DEVELOPMENT

Editor: K. J. Hanford

Editorial address:
Overseas Development Administration
Foreign and Commonwealth Office
Eland House
Stag Place
London S.W. 1, England

Sponsor: same as above

Frequency: BM
Subscription: 57s individual; 35s student

Founded: 1966
Subscribers: 1,000

Editorial interest:
Chronological: unrestricted
Geographical: Africa, Asia, Canada, Latin America, Middle East, United
States, West Indies

OVERSEAS DEVELOPMENT (cont'd)

> Topical: agriculture, anthropology, communications media, cultural affairs, demography, economics, politics and government, research methods, science and technology, social history, sociology, transportation
> Special scope: development

Editorial policies:
> Query prior to submission of ms. optional
> Style manual: none prescribed
> Preferred length of ms.: 1,000 words maximum; no serialization
> Author payment: six article reprints
> End notes. Accepts mss. and publishes articles in English. Wants mss. on development and technical assistance to emerging countries and on experiences of persons working in the field.

PAN-AFRICAN JOURNAL

Editor: Maina Kagombe

Editorial address:
> 675 West End Avenue, Suite 2D
> New York, New York 10025

Sponsor: Pan-African Institute, Inc.

Frequency: Q

Subscription: $15

Founded: 1968

Subscribers: 1,500

Editorial interest:
> Chronological: 1900 to present, current events
> Geographical: Africa (mainly), Latin America, United States, West Indies
> Topical: agriculture, anthropology, auxiliary historical disciplines, bibliographical articles, cultural affairs, demography, discovery and exploration, economics, education, ethnology, folklore, foreign relations, geography, historiography, history of ideas, international organizations, legal and constitutional affairs, literature (history and criticism), medicine (history), military affairs, music (history), philosophy, philosophy of history, politics and government, research methods, social history, sociology
> Special scope: Swahili poetry, creative short stories

Editorial policies:
> Query prior to submission of ms. optional
> Style manual: Kate L. Turabian, *A Manual for Writers*
> Preferred length of ms.: 10-16 typed pages; longer articles for serialization considered on merit
> Author payment: 25 article reprints
> End notes. Accepts mss. and publishes articles in English, but will accept poetry in Swahili. Potential authors should write for an academic and university level audience. Wants original, creative mss. with an

PAN-AFRICAN JOURNAL (cont'd)

Afrocentric approach to African affairs tending to search for change. Also welcomes reinterpretations of literature written by non-Africans, especially Europeans on Africa, and mss. on the history of ideas and politics and government dealing with African affairs.

Notes: Articles abstracted or indexed in CC, HA, SSHI
   Special features: commentary on current and controversial issues. Book reviews are solicited, but freelance offerings are considered; remuneration in offprints or copy of issue in which review appears. Wants critical reviews two to four typed pages in length. Persons interested in reviewing should contact the editor.

PAPERS IN INTERNATIONAL STUDIES: Africa Series

Editor: Dr. Bob J. Walter

Editorial address:
   Center for International Studies
   Ohio University
   Athens, Ohio 45701

Sponsor: same as above

Frequency: irr.
Subscription: serial; charged by paper
   when shipped

Founded: 1968
Subscribers: 58

Editorial interest:
   Chronological: unrestricted
   Geographical: Africa
   Topical: unrestricted

Editorial policies:
   Query prior to submission of ms.
   Preferred length of ms.: 30-60 typed pages; no serialization
   Author payment: 10 copies of issue, can purchase others at 20% discount
   Bottom notes. Potential authors should write for an audience of scholars and serious students of the area. Would like to see articles on almost anything in the cultural field, especially on Arab North Africa, and on South Africa (sociology in particular).

Notes: A monograph series. Reports on submissions in six weeks to two months.

PHYLON: The Atlanta University Review of Race and Culture

Editor: John D. Reid

Associate editor: Mrs. Lucy C. Grigsby

Editorial address:
Atlanta University
223 Chestnut Street, S.W.
Atlanta, Georgia 30314

Sponsor: same as above

Frequency: Q
Subscription: $7.00 U.S.; $8 elsewhere

Founded: 1940
Subscribers: 2,200

Editorial interest:
Chronological: unrestricted
Geographical: worldwide
Topical: anthropology, art, auxiliary historical disciplines, bibliographical articles, cultural affairs, education, ethnology, folklore, literature (history and criticism), social history, sociology
Special scope: race and culture

Editorial policies:
Style manual: Chicago
Preferred length of ms.: 10-20 typed pages; no serialization
Author payment: 20 article reprints
Bottom or end notes. Authors should write for a sophisticated, worldwide audience.

Notes: Articles abstracted or indexed in AHL, HA, PA, PAIS, SSHI. Authors should submit the original and one copy of their mss. Book reviews are assigned, but occasionally accepts freelance offerings; no remuneration.

PRESENCE AFRICAINE

Editor: Alioune Diop

Editorial address:
42 rue Descartes
75 Paris 5e, France

Sponsor: Société Africaine de Culture

Frequency: Q
Subscription: Fr 25

Founded: 1947
Subscribers: 1,600

Editorial interest:
Chronological: unrestricted
Geographical: Africa and Blacks in Canada, United States, and West Indies
Topical: agriculture, anthropology, archaeology, architecture, auxiliary historical disciplines, bibliographical articles, church or ecclesiastical affairs, communications media, cultural affairs, demography, discovery and exploration, economics, education, ethnology,

PRESENCE AFRICAINE (cont'd)

folklore, foreign relations, frontier areas, geography, historiography, history of ideas, international law, international organizations, language (philology, semantics), legal and constitutional affairs, literature (history and criticism), maritime history, medicine (history), military affairs, music (history), philosophy, philosophy of history, politics and government, religious studies, research methods, science and technology, social history, sociology, theatre and drama, transportation

Editorial policies:

Query prior to submission of ms.

Style manual: none

Preferred length of ms.: varies according to subject, usually 15-30 typed pages; serialization rare

Author payment: Fr 15 per printed page, one copy of issue in which article appears, and article reprints at cost if ordered in advance

Bottom notes, consecutively numbered. Address mss. to Monsieur Kala-Lobe. Potential authors should write for an audience of African intellectuals and specialists. *Presence Africaine* "is a cultural quarterly rather than one of mass appeal."

Notes: Mss. should be double-spaced with adequate margins and typed on good quality paper. Potential authors should insure that their names and addresses are on the mss. and on the backs of envelopes. Attention should be paid to chapter headings and sub-headings; adequate spaces should be left between these and opening lines of the text. Book reviews are assigned, but freelance offerings are considered; Fr 12 per printed page remuneration. Editorial reports on submissions in three to six months.

QUARTERLY JOURNAL OF ADMINISTRATION

Editors: Adekayo Adedeji, Colin Baker, and Kolawole Adelaja

Editorial address:
P.M.B. 5246
Ibadan, Nigeria

Sponsor: Institute of Administration, University of Ife

Frequency: Q   Founded: 1966
Subscription: N£1   Subscribers: 600

Editorial interest:

Chronological: unrestricted (current events emphasis)

Geographical: Africa

Topical: economics, foreign relations, international organizations, legal and constitutional affairs, politics and government (mostly), research methods

QUARTERLY JOURNAL OF ADMINISTRATION (cont'd)

Editorial policies:
> Style manual: none prescribed
> Preferred length of ms.: 4,000-6,000 words; would consider longer
> articles for serialization
> Author payment: 20 article reprints
> Bottom notes. Mss. accepted and articles published in English only.
> Potential authors should write for an audience of scholars and
> senior practitioners of public administration and management.
> Prefer articles on comparative studies of government in the develop-
> ing world; studies in depth of the functioning and structure of
> governmental organization.

Notes:
> Special features: "Administrative Notes," "Notes on Government Publi-
> cations." Book reviews are assigned, but freelance offerings con-
> sidered; no remuneration. Reports on submissions in two to eight
> weeks.

RACE: A Journal of Race and Group Relations

Editor: Simon Abbott

Editorial address:
> 247-9 Pentonville Road
> London N.1, England

Sponsor: Institute of Race Relations

Frequency: Q   Founded: 1958
Subscription: $12.50/£4.50   Subscribers: 1,500

Editorial interest:
> Chronological: unrestricted
> Geographical: worldwide
> Topical: anthropology, communications media, economics, education,
> ethnology, folklore, foreign relations, history of ideas, legal and
> constitutional affairs, politics and government, research methods,
> social history, sociology
> Special scope: race and group relations

Editorial policies:
> Query prior to submission of ms.
> Style manual: Hart's *Rules* (Oxford University Press); style sheet avail-
> able on request
> Preferred length of ms.: 4,000-6,000 words; articles for serialization
> occasionally considered
> Author payment: 25 article reprints
> End notes, textual elucidation, and comment at foot of page. Articles
> should adopt a multidisciplinary academic approach. Research
> should be original, the findings clearly expressed, and tables and
> sub-headings included where necessary. Conclusions, particularly

RACE (cont'd)

regarding policy or research methods, should be drawn. Welcomes research-based but policy-oriented structural change studies of race and group relations.

Notes: Articles abstracted or indexed in AA, *British Humanities Index*, CC, PA, PAIS, *Race Relations Abstracts*, SA

Special features: "Quarterly Forum," which includes discussion of research, methods, and problems, and reports on conferences and organizations of interest to students of race relations. Authors should submit two copies of ms. Potential contributors are advised to study previous issues before submitting ms. Book reviews are normally assigned, but potential reviewers are invited to contact the editor. Freelance offerings are occasionally accepted; no remuneration.

RACE RELATIONS NEWS

Editor: R. M. de Villiers

Editorial address:
South African Institute of Race Relations
P.O. Box 97
Johannesburg, South Africa

Sponsor: same as above

Frequency: M   Founded: 1933
Subscription: Rds 1/$1.41 plus postage   Subscribers: 4,600

Editorial interest:
Chronological: current events
Geographical: South Africa
Topical: sociology
Special scope: race relations

Editorial policies:
Query prior to submission of ms.
Style manual: none prescribed
Preferred length of ms.: 500-800 words
Author payment: six copies of issue in which article appears
End notes. Accepts mss. and publishes articles in Afrikaans or English. Articles should be directed to an academic, diplomatic, and business audience. Wants mss. on current race relations in South Africa.

Notes: Book reviews are staff written. Editorial decision on submissions within four to six weeks. Illustrated.

RENAISSANCE 2: A Journal of Afro-American Studies

Editor: Alric B. Nembhard

Managing editor: M. Teresa McAlpine

Editorial address:
>84 Yale Station
>New Haven, Connecticut 06520

Sponsor: Afro-American Cultural Center at Yale University

Frequency: SA   Founded: 1972
Subscription: $3.50 in U.S.; $4.25 in
>Canada; $4.50 elsewhere

Editorial interest:
>Chronological: unrestricted
>Geographical: Africa, United States, West Indies
>Topical: art, cultural affairs, education, folklore, history of ideas, literature, music, politics and government, religious studies, sociology

Editorial policies:
>Query prior to submission of ms.
>Style manual: Chicago
>Preferred length of ms.: 1,000-6,000 words; no serialization
>End notes. Editor welcomes mss. "on the Black experience presenting scholarly and creative articles on Blacks throughout the world."

RESEARCH IN AFRICAN LITERATURES

Editor: Bernth Lindfors

Editorial address:
>African and Afro-American Research Institute
>University of Texas
>2609 University Avenue, 314
>Austin, Texas 78712

Sponsors: African Literature Committee of the African Studies Association of America and the African Literatures Seminar of the Modern Language Association

Frequency: SA   Founded: 1970
Subscription: free to subscribers in Africa,   Circulation: 1,500
>Eastern Europe, South and Central
>America; $6.00 for others

Editorial interest:
>Chronological: unrestricted
>Geographical: Africa
>Topical: bibliographical articles, cinema and film, folklore, history of ideas, literature (history), research methods, theatre and drama
>Special scope: discovery, filmography, oral literature

RESEARCH IN AFRICAN LITERATURES (cont'd)

Editorial policies:
>
> Style manual: MLA Style Sheet
>
> Preferred length of ms.: unrestricted; accepts articles for serialization
>
> Author payment: 45 article reprints
>
> End notes. Accepts mss. and publishes articles in English or French. Wants well-written theoretical, historical, and bibliographical mss. "Literary criticism, translations, creative writing and unanalyzed collections of folklore texts are not desired."

Notes: Articles abstracted in AES, AFS, SSHI
>
> Special features: research in progress, library and archive reports, conference reports, new publications. Book reviews are assigned and solicited, but freelance offerings are considered; no remuneration

REVIEW OF BLACK POLITICAL ECONOMY

Editor: Alvin Puryear

Editorial address:
>
> 112 West 120th Street
>
> New York, New York 10027

Sponsor: Black Economic Research Center

Frequency: Q   Founded: 1970
Subscription: $7   Subscribers: 2,000

Editorial interest:
>
> Chronological: current events
>
> Geographical: Africa, South America (Black areas), United States, West Indies
>
> Topical: agriculture, business, church or ecclesiastical affairs, communications media, economics, education, foreign relations, international organizations, politics and government, research methods, science and technology

Editorial policies:
>
> Query prior to submission of ms.
>
> Style manual: Marjorie E. Skillen, *et al.*, *Words into Type* (Appleton-Century-Crofts)
>
> Preferred length of ms.: 25 typed pages; longer articles accepted for serialization
>
> Author payment: eight article reprints
>
> Accepts mss. and publishes articles in English. Potential authors should write for an audience of economists, political scientists, and informed laymen. Wants mss. dealing with economics of Blacks.

Notes: Book reviews are assigned and solicited, but freelance offerings are welcome; no remuneration. Persons interested in reviewing should contact the editor. Editorial reports on submissions within six weeks.

RHODESIA AGRICULTURAL JOURNAL

Editor: W. B. Cleghorn

Editorial address:
Department of Research and Specialist Services
P.O. Box 8108
Causeway, Salisbury, Rhodesia

Sponsor: Ministry of Agriculture

Frequency: BM
Subscription: 1.25 Rhodesia pounds

Founded: 1903
Subscribers: 2,000

Editorial interest:
Chronological: current events
Geographical: Rhodesia (mainly), tropical Southern Africa
Topical: agriculture

Editorial policies:
Style manual: "Instruction for the Preparation of Papers" published in
each issue
Preferred length of ms.: 3,600 words; longer articles for serialization
accepted
Author payment: 20 Rhodesian pounds maximum, and 25 article
reprints
Accepts mss. and publishes articles in English. Potential authors should
write for a sophisticated audience of workers in field husbandry,
animal husbandry, and pasture and range development; also for
extension personnel who serve the unsophisticated peasant farmer
of Africa.

Notes: Articles abstracted or indexed in CC, *Current Agricultural Serials*,
International Abstract of Biological Science, and *Tobacco Abstracts*.
Book reviews are solicited; remuneration. Editorial reports on sub-
missions in one month.

RHODESIA AND WORLD REPORT

Editor: Dr. Ian G. Anderson

Editorial address:
P.O. Box 1871
Salisbury, Rhodesia

Sponsor: Candour League of Rhodesia

Frequency: M
Subscription: $3.50/£1.13

Founded: 1966
Subscribers: 5,000

Editorial interest:
Chronological: current events
Geographical: Southern Africa, Rhodesia
Topical: politics and government

RHODESIA AND WORLD REPORT (cont'd)

Editorial policies:

> The *Report* produces most of their own material and welcomes extraneous contributions only from contributors known to and vouched for by them.
>
> No author payment.
>
> Potential authors should write constructive conservatism for a conservative audience. Editorial policy is "to disseminate information about the general assault on European influence in Southern Africa, especially in Rhodesia."

Notes: Articles abstracted in *Current Affairs*. They do their own book reviewing, but welcome books for review. Reports on submissions as soon as possible.

RHODESIAN JOURNAL OF ECONOMICS

Editor: A. M. Hawkins

Editorial address:
Private Bag 167H
Mount Pleasant, Salisbury, Rhodesia

Sponsor: Rhodesian Economic Society

Frequency: Q
Subscription: $4.80

Founded: 1967
Subscribers: approximately 300

Editorial interest:
> Chronological: 1900 to present, current events
> Geographical: Africa
> Topical: agriculture, business, economics, education

Editorial policies:
> Style manual: none prescribed
> Preferred length of ms.: 3,000-6,000 words; longer articles for serialization accepted
> Author payment: two copies of issue in which article appears
> Bottom or end notes. Accepts mss. and publishes articles in English. Potential authors should write for an academic and business audience. Wants mss. on applied economics in the African field.

Notes:
> Special feature: diary of events of economic importance. Potential contributors are urged to restrict the amount of graphical and tabular material and to write in simple, lucid English with a minimum of jargon. Few book reviews. Editorial reports on submissions within one month.

ROCZNIK ORIENTALISTYCZNY

Editor-in-chief: Jan Reychman

Secretary: Edward Tryjarski

Editorial board: Janusz Chmielewski, Stanisaw Kaysynski, Wiesaw Kotanski, Tadeusz Lewicki, and Eugeniusz Suszkiewicz

Editorial address:
  Warszawa 10
  Grojecka 17, Room 111
  Polska

Sponsor: Polska Akademia Nauk—Komitet Nauk Orientalistycznych (Polish Academy of Sciences—Oriental Committee)

Frequency: SA   Founded: 1915
                                       Circulation: 500

Editorial interest:
  Chronological: unrestricted
  Geographical: Africa, Asia, Eastern Europe, Far East, Middle East, Russia/USSR, West Indies
  Topical: anthropology, archaeology, art, ethnology, folklore, geography, historiography, history of ideas, language (philology, semantics), literature (history and criticism), medicine (history), philosophy, religious studies, social history, theatre and drama

Editorial policies:
  Preferred length of ms.: 20 typed pages; longer articles sometimes accepted for serialization
  Author payment: cash, and 20 off-prints
  End notes preferred, but bottom notes accepted. Accepts and publishes articles in English, French, German, Russian, or (rarely) Polish. Potential authors should write for an audience of scholars. Would like to see articles presenting new ideas in an intelligible form.

Notes: Articles abstracted or indexed in HA, *Orientalistische Literaturzeitung*. Freelance book reviews accepted; paid as articles. Book reviews should be sent to the members of the editorial board or the secretary. Reports on submissions vary from a few weeks to a few months.

ROUND TABLE: The Commonwealth Journal of International Affairs

Editor: Robert Jackson

Editorial address:
  18 Northumberland Avenue
  London, W.C.2, England

Frequency: Q   Founded: 1910
Subscription: £4/$10

Editorial interest:
  Chronological: 1900 to present

ROUND TABLE (cont'd)

Geographical: Africa, Asia, Canada, Commonwealth (British), Latin America, Middle East, Pacific Area, Russia/USSR, United States, Western Europe

Topical: agriculture, air forces, business, communications media, cultural affairs, economics, education, foreign relations (mostly), international organizations, legal and constitutional affairs, military affairs (mostly), naval affairs (mostly), politics and government (mostly)

Editorial policies:

Query prior to submission of ms.

Style manual: none prescribed

Preferred length of ms.: 4,000 words; no serialization

Author payment: cash rate varies

Bottom notes. Articles must be written for an elite audience of men in public affairs, many of whom are in academic life. Interested in studies of international affairs from a Commonwealth perspective.

Notes: Articles abstracted in AHL, HA. Prospective authors should study past issues for familiarization with contents. Review articles are assigned; remuneration as for articles.

RURAL AFRICANA

Editor: Norman N. Miller

Editorial address:

African Studies Center
Michigan State University
East Lansing, Michigan 48823

Sponsor: same as above

Frequency: Q

Subscription: $4.50 individual; $9 institutional

Founded: 1967

Subscribers: approximately 250

Editorial interest:

Chronological: unrestricted

Geographical: Africa (south of the Sahara)

Topical: agriculture, anthropology, archaeology, architecture, auxiliary historical disciplines, bibliographical articles, business, church or ecclesiastical affairs, communications media, cultural affairs, demography, discovery and exploration, economics, education, ethnology, foreign relations, geography, historiography, history of ideas, international organizations, legal and constitutional affairs, maritime history, medicine (history), military affairs, politics and government, research methods, science and technology, social history, sociology, transportation

Special scope: social and economic development of rural Africa south of the Sahara

RURAL AFRICANA (cont'd)

Editorial policies:
> Query letter prior to submission of ms., since all mss. are solicited by guest editors
> Style manual: Chicago or *American Anthropologist*
> Preferred length of ms.: 15-30 typed pages; no serialization to date
> Author payment: $50 honorarium to guest editor; four article reprints to contributors
> Bibliographical reference notes at end of ms., explanatory notes at bottom of page. Solicits mss. and publishes articles in English.

Notes:
> Special features: news items, research reports, and comprehensive bibliographies. No book reviews.

SCHOOL OF ORIENTAL AND AFRICAN STUDIES BULLETIN

Chairman of the editorial board: Edward Ullendorff, F.B.A.

Editorial secretary: Miss D. M. Johnson

Editorial address:
> School of Oriental and African Studies
> London University
> London, W.C.1, England

Sponsor: same as above

Frequency: TA

Founded: 1917

Subscription: £12

Subscribers: 2,000

Editorial interest:
> Chronological: unrestricted
> Geographical: Africa, Asia, Middle East, Pacific Area
> Topical: agriculture, anthropology, archaeology, architecture, auxiliary historical disciplines, bibliographical articles, church or ecclesiastical affairs, cultural affairs, demography, discovery and exploration, ethnology, folklore, geography, historiography, history of ideas, language (philology, semantics), legal and constitutional affairs, literature (history and criticism), medicine (history), music (history), philosophy, philosophy of history, religious studies, theatre and drama

Editorial policies:
> Style manual: consult previous issues
> Preferred length of ms.: 2,000-20,000 words; serialization possible in special cases
> Author payment: 25 article reprints, more at cost to author
> Bottom notes. Accepts mss. and publishes articles in English, French, German, and occasionally Italian. Address mss. to the editorial secretary. Potential authors should write for a highly specialized audience in Oriental and African studies.

Notes: Book reviews are assigned; no remuneration.

SECOND ORDER: An African Journal of Philosophy

Editor: Professor J. O. Sodipo

Associate editors: Vernon Pratt and J. S. Wiredu

Editorial address:
Department of Philosophy
University of Ife
Ile-Ife, Nigeria

Sponsor: University of Ife

Frequency: SA

Subscription: $3.70 in Nigeria; $5.60
elsewhere; $2.50 institutional in
Nigeria; $3.80 institutional elsewhere

Founded: 1970 (first issue—
January 1972)
Subscribers: approximately
400

Editorial interest:
Chronological: unrestricted
Geographical: worldwide (special emphasis upon Africa)
Topical: anthropology, history of ideas, philosophy, philosophy of
history, religious studies, sociology

Editorial policies:
Style manual: none prescribed
Preferred length of ms.: 3,000-5,000 words; accepts articles for
serialization
Author payment: 20 article reprints
End notes. Prefers good philosophical articles.

Notes: Articles indexed in SSHI. Book reviews are solicited, although freelance contributions are accepted. Editorial response to submissions
within six months.

SEPIA MAGAZINE

Editor: Ben Burns

Editorial address:
75 East Wacker Drive
Chicago, Illinois 60601

Sponsor: Good Publishing Co.

Frequency: M
Subscription: $6

Founded: 1951
Circulation: 102,000

Editorial interest:
Chronological: current events
Geographical: Africa, Latin America, United States, West Indies
Topical: business, church or ecclesiastical affairs, cinema and film,
cultural affairs, economics, education, politics and government,
social history, sociology, theatre and drama

SEPIA MAGAZINE (cont'd)

Editorial policies:
>Query prior to submission of ms.
>Preferred length of ms.: 3,000 words; no serialization
>Author payment: $150
>Potential authors should write for a mass audience. Would like to see current reports on Black life in the United States.

Notes: No book reviews. Reports on submissions in one week.

SIERRA LEONE STUDIES

Editor: John Peterson

Editorial address:
>Department of Modern History
>Fourah Bay College
>University of Sierra Leone
>Freetown, Sierra Leone

Sponsor: Sierra Leone University Press

Frequency: SA
Subscription: Leone 3.00 in West Africa; $4.50/£1.50 elsewhere

Founded: 1918
Subscribers: 250

Editorial interest:
>Chronological: unrestricted
>Geographical: Africa, Sierra Leone, West Africa
>Topical: unrestricted

Editorial policies:
>Style manual: MLA Style Sheet
>Preferred length of ms.: 5,000 words; longer articles for serialization considered
>Author payment: six article reprints
>End notes. Accepts mss. in any language, but prefers English. Publishes articles in English. Wants mss. on the sciences, literature, or social sciences relating to Sierra Leone and West Africa.

Notes: Articles abstracted in HA
>Special feature: research notes. Book reviews are assigned; no remuneration. Persons interested in reviewing should contact the editor. Editorial reports on submissions generally within four weeks.

SOCIETE DES AFRICANISTES JOURNAL

Editorial address:
>Musée de L.Homme
>Place du Trocadero
>75, Paris 16e, France

Sponsor: same as above

SOCIETE DES AFRICANISTES JOURNAL (cont'd)

Frequency: SA   Founded: 1931
Subscription: Fr 55   Subscribers: 510

Editorial interest:
Chronological: unrestricted
Geographical: Africa
Topical: agriculture, anthropology, archaeology, architecture, art,
auxiliary historical disciplines, bibliographical articles, economics,
ethnology, language (philology, semantics), music (history),
religious studies, social history, sociology

Editorial policies:
Style manual: none prescribed
Preferred length of ms.: 30 typed pages; longer articles for serializa-
tion accepted
Author payment: 25 article reprints
Bottom notes. Accepts mss. and publishes articles in English, French, or
German. Address mss. to the secrétariat.

Notes:
Special feature: bibliography. Persons interested in book reviewing
should contact the secrétariat. Editorial reports on submissions in
about one month.

SOCIETY OF MALAWI JOURNAL

Editor: G. D. Hayes

Editorial address:
Box 5135
Limbe, Malawi

Sponsor: Historical and Scientific Society of Malawi

Frequency: SA   Founded: 1948 (as *Nyasaland*
Subscription: 15s/1.5 Malawi pounds   *Journal*)
per issue   Subscribers: approximately
                                           500

Editorial interest:
Chronological: unrestricted
Geographical: Malawi
Topical: agriculture, anthropology, archaeology, architecture, art,
auxiliary historical disciplines, bibliographical articles, business,
communications media, cultural affairs, discovery and exploration, ethnology, folklore, geography, historiography, medicine
(history), military affairs, music (history), naval affairs, religious
studies, science and technology

Editorial policies:
Query prior to submission of ms.
Style manual: any scholarly style
Preferred length of ms.: 5,000-10,000 words; no serialization

SOCIETY OF MALAWI JOURNAL (cont'd)

Author payment: 10 article reprints
Bottom notes. Accepts mss. and publishes articles in English. Wants mss. on geography, history, archaeology, anthropology, agriculture, and natural history relating to Malawi

Notes: Articles abstracted in HA. Book reviews are assigned; no remuneration.

SOUTH AFRICAN ARCHAEOLOGICAL BULLETIN

Editors: R. R. Inskeep and R. F. Summers

Editorial address:
P.O. Box 31
Claremont Cape, South Africa

Sponsor: South African Archaeological Society

Frequency: SA   Founded: 1945
Subscription: Rds 5

Editorial interest:
Chronological: pre-history to nineteenth century
Geographical: Africa (occasional review articles on non-African regions)
Topical: archaeology, ethnology, research methods

Editorial policies:
Query prior to submission of ms.
Style manual: "Instructions to Authors" printed in every issue
Preferred length of ms.: varies with topic; no serialization
Author payment: no cash remuneration; subventions are sometimes solicited from authors; 25 tearsheet copies of article
Reference notes should be in the text between separating lines. Accepts mss. and publishes articles in English. Wants mss. presenting definitive research reports, methodology and philosophy, and review articles.

Notes: Book reviews are solicited; no remuneration. Persons interested in reviewing should contact the review editor at the editorial address. Editorial decision on submissions in two months.

SOUTH AFRICAN GEOGRAPHICAL JOURNAL

Editors: T. J. D. Fair and P. D. Tyson

Editorial address:
South African Geographical Society
P.O. Box 31201
Braamfontein, South Africa

Sponsor: same as above

Frequency: A   Founded: 1917
Subscription: Rds 4   Subscribers: 500

SOUTH AFRICAN GEOGRAPHICAL JOURNAL (cont'd)

Editorial interest:
>   Chronological: unrestricted
>   Geographical: Africa
>   Topical: agriculture, demography, economics, education, geography,
>   transportation
>   Special scope: climatology

Editorial policies:
>   Style manual: own house style, consult journal for "Notes to Authors"
>   Preferred length of ms.: 5,000 words; no serialization
>   Author payment: none
>   Textual notes at bottom of page, reference notes at end. Accepts mss.
>   and publishes articles in Afrikaans or English. Potential authors
>   should write for an audience of professional geographers. "Wants
>   articles of a suitably high standard related to academic geography
>   preferably at university level."

Notes: Articles abstracted or indexed in *Annotated World List of Selected
Current Geographical Serials in English*. Freelance book reviews are
accepted; no remuneration. Editorial reports on submissions in two to
three months.

SOUTH AFRICAN LAW JOURNAL

Editor: Ellison Kahn

Editorial address:
>   Dean of the School of Law
>   University of Witwatersrand
>   Jan Smuts Avenue
>   Johannesburg, South Africa

Frequency: Q   Founded: 1884
Subscription: Rds 9.75   Subscribers: 2,100

Editorial interest:
>   Chronological: current events
>   Geographical: Africa, South Africa
>   Topical: international law, legal and constitutional affairs

Editorial policies:
>   Style manual: house style booklet available on request
>   Preferred length of ms.: 25 typed pages maximum; longer articles for
>   serialization accepted
>   Author payment: Rds 2 per printed page, and two copies of issue in
>   which article appears; article reprints supplied on request
>   Bottom or end notes. Accepts mss. and publishes articles in Afrikaans or
>   English. Potential contributors should write for lawyers and law
>   students. Wants mss. on legal subjects only.

Notes:
>   Special feature: recent court decisions. Book reviews are assigned; no
>   remuneration. Editorial reports on submissions in two months.

SOUTH WEST AFRICAN SCIENTIFIC SOCIETY NEWSLETTER

Editor: H. J. Rust

Editorial address:
S.W.A. Scientific Society
P.O. Box 67
Windhoek, South West Africa

Sponsor: South West African Scientific Society

Frequency: M

Founded: 1959

Subscription: Rds 4 (includes *Journal*)

Subscribers: approximately 650

Editorial interest:
Chronological: unrestricted
Geographical: Africa
Topical: anthropology, archaeology, bibliographical articles, ethnology, geography, literature (history and criticism)
Special scope: South West Africa

Editorial policies:
Query prior to submission of ms.
Style manual: none prescribed
Preferred length of ms.: 2-7 typed pages
Author payment: 10 copies of *Newsletter* in which article appears
Bottom notes. Accepts mss. and publishes articles in Afrikaans, English, or German. Wants articles of a scientific nature.

Notes: Indexed in CC
Special feature: bibliography. Editorial decision on submissions within one month.

SPEAR

Editor: Tony Momoh

Editorial address:
3-7 Kakawa Street
Lagos, Nigeria

Sponsor: Daily Times of Nigeria, Limited

Frequency: M

Founded: 1962

Subscription: N£1/3 surface; N£4/4 airmail

Subscribers: 500

Editorial interest:
Chronological: current events
Geographical: Africa
Topical: unrestricted

Editorial policies:
Preferred length of ms.: six typed pages; accepts longer articles for serialization
Author payment: cash payment varies; one copy of issue in which article appears

SPEAR (cont'd)

Bottom or end notes. Accepts mss. and publishes articles in English only. Seeks articles that have a broad appeal and that are of interest to the general public.

Notes: Book reviews are assigned. Persons interested in reviewing should write the editor. Reports on submissions in two weeks.

SPECULUM: A Journal of Mediaeval Studies

Editor: Paul Meyvaert

Assistant editors: Giles Constable, Larry D. Benson, and Theodore M. Andersson

Editorial address:
The Mediaeval Academy of America
1430 Massachusetts Avenue
Cambridge, Massachusetts 02138

Sponsor: same as above

Frequency: Q

Founded: 1926

Subscription: $18 individual; $21 institutional

Subscribers: 4,988

Editorial interest:
Chronological: 500-1500 A.D.
Geographical: Africa, Eastern Europe, Middle East, Russia, Scandinavia, Western Europe
Topical: architecture, art, auxiliary historical disciplines, economics, geography, historiography, literature (history and criticism), music (history), philosophy, philosophy of history, science and technology, social history

Editorial policies:
Style manual: MLA Style Sheet
Preferred length of ms.: unspecified; no serialization
Author payment: none
End notes. Wants scholarly articles on the Middle Ages.

Notes: Articles indexed in *Art Index*, SSHI
Special features: "Books Received," "Bibliography of American Periodical Literature." Authors should check previous issues for special conventions. Book reviews are assigned (99%).

SPRINGBOK

Editor: Theo. E. G. Cutten

Editorial address:
Duncan House
11 de Villiers Street
Johannesburg, South Africa

SPRINGBOK (cont'd)

Sponsor: South African Legion

Frequency: M
Subscription: Rds 2

Founded: 1921
Subscribers: 12,000

Editorial interest:
   Chronological: 1900 to present
   Geographical: Africa, Western Europe
   Topical: air forces, military affairs, naval affairs
   Special scope: matters of interest to South African ex-servicemen and
      national servicemen

Editorial policies:
   Query prior to submission of ms.
   Style manual: none prescribed
   Preferred length of ms.: not reported
   Author payment: none
   Reference notes should be integrated into the text. Contributors must
      be members of the South African Legion. Accepts mss. and
      publishes articles in Afrikaans or English. Potential authors
      should write for a military and ex-service audience.

Notes: Articles are cited in CC. Editor reports that contributions exceed available space. Book reviews are assigned; no remuneration.

STUDIA MUSICOLOGIA: Academiae Scientiarum Hungaricae

Editor: B. Szabolsci

Managing editor: Z. Falvy

Editorial address:
   I. Országház-u.9.
   Budapest, Hungary

Sponsor: Hungarian Academy of Sciences

Frequency: 9 xy
Subscription: $24

Founded: 1961

Editorial interest:
   Chronological: 1100 to the present
   Geographical: Africa, Asia, Balkans, Eastern Europe, Russia/USSR,
      Western Europe
   Topical: music (history)

Editorial policies:
   Query prior to submission of ms.
   Style manual: none prescribed; consult previous issues
   Preferred length of ms.: unspecified
   Author payment: 100 article reprints
   Accepts mss. and publishes articles in English, French, German, Italian,
      or Russian

Notes: Articles cited in *Music Index*. No further information reported.

STUDIA ORIENTALIA

Editor: Hmari Kärki

Editorial address:
Snellmanink - 9-11
Helsinki 17, Finland

Sponsor: Societas Orientalis Fennica

Frequency: 1-2 volumes yearly
Subscription: $10-$25

Founded: 1922
Subscribers: 46

Editorial interest:
Chronological: unrestricted
Geographical: Africa, Asia, Middle East
Special scope: Assyriology, Islamistics

Editorial policies:
Preferred length of ms.: maximum of 250 typed pages; longer articles
are accepted for serialization
Author payment: 30 complimentary reprints of article
Bottom notes. Mss. are accepted and published in English, French, or
German. Potential authors should write for a scholarly audience.

STUDIES IN AFRICAN LINGUISTICS

Editor: Talmy Giuón

Editorial address:
Department of Linguistics
University of California
Los Angeles, California 90024

Sponsor: African Studies Center, University of California, Los Angeles

Frequency: TA
Subscription: $7 in U.S. and Canada;
$8 elsewhere

Founded: 1970
Subscribers: 170

Editorial interest:
Chronological: unrestricted
Geographical: Africa
Topical: language
Special scope: linguistics

Editorial policies:
Query prior to submission of ms. optional
Style manual: own house style, consult previous issues or follow
Linguistic Society of America style sheet
Preferred length of ms.: 60 typed pages maximum; longer articles for
serialization might be considered
Author payment: 50 article reprints

STUDIES IN AFRICAN LINGUISTICS (cont'd)

End notes. Accepts mss. and publishes articles in English. Potential authors should write for an audience of professional linguists. Wants mss. with theoretical orientation (i.e., linguistic theory).

Notes:

Special feature: occasional supplements. No book reviews.

STUDIES IN BLACK LITERATURE

Editor: Raman K. Singh

Editorial address:
Box 3425
College Station
Fredericksburg, Virginia 22401

Frequency: TA

Subscription: $4 individual; $7 institutional

Founded: 1970

Subscribers: approximately 225

Editorial interest:
Chronological: unrestricted
Geographical: Africa, United States, West Indies
Topical: folklore, literature (history and criticism), theatre and drama
Special scope: literature of Afro-Americans, Africans, and Caribbeans

Editorial policies:
Style manual: MLA Style Sheet
Preferred length of ms.: 10 typed pages; longer articles accepted for serialization
Author payment: two copies of issue in which article appears
End notes. Accepts mss. and publishes articles in English. Potential authors should write for students and teachers of literature as well as the educated man of letters. Wants mss. that offer a bold, objective analysis, interpretation, and criticism of Black literature dealing with the modern period.

Notes: Articles abstracted or indexed in AES, PMLA
Special feature: bibliographies of Black literature. Book reviews are few and being phased out. Editorial reports on submissions in three to eight weeks.

STUDIES IN RACE AND NATIONS

Editor: Tilden J. LeMelle

Managing editor: Gail S. Schoettler

Editorial address:
Center on International Race Relations
Graduate School of International Studies
University of Denver
Denver, Colorado 80210

STUDIES IN RACE AND NATIONS (cont'd)

Sponsor: same as above

Frequency: Q   Founded: 1969
Subscription: $7   Subscribers: 126

Editorial interest:
  Chronological: unrestricted
  Geographical: Africa, United States, Western Europe
  Topical: cultural affairs, economics, foreign relations, history of ideas, international law, international organizations, legal and constitutional affairs, military affairs, politics and government, research methods, social history, sociology
  Special scope: race and international relations, racial conflict

Editorial policies:
  Query preferred prior to submission of ms.
  Style manual: MLA Style Sheet
  Preferred length of ms.: 15,000-40,000 words; serialization acceptable
  Author payment: 10 article reprints
  End notes. Articles should be directed to an audience of academics and educated readers. Desires mss. that are theoretical and/or issue- or problem-oriented concerning race and international relations; race and U.S. foreign policy.

Notes: Cited in SSHI. No book reviews. Editorial decisions on submissions within one month.

STUDIES ON DEVELOPING COUNTRIES

Editor-in-chief: József Bognar

Editor: Mrs. Mária Köszegi

Editorial address:
  P.O. Box 36
  Budapest 126, Hungary

Sponsor: Center for Afro-Asian Research, Hungarian Academy of Science

Frequency: irr.   Founded: 1965
Subscription: varies

Editorial interest:
  Chronological: unrestricted (current emphasis)
  Geographical: Asia, Africa, Latin America, Middle East, Pacific Area, West Indies
  Topical: agriculture, auxiliary historical disciplines, economics, ethnology, foreign relations, politics and government, social history, sociology
  Special scope: economic and social problems of developing countries

STUDIES ON DEVELOPING COUNTRIES (cont'd)

Editorial policies:
>Query prior to submission of ms.
>Style manual: none prescribed
>Preferred length of ms.: 32-64 typed pages; no serialization
>Author payment: 10 article reprints
>End notes. Accepts mss. and publishes articles in English, French, German, Hungarian, Russian, or Spanish. Potential authors should write for a scholarly and learned audience. Wants mss. on the economic and social problems of developing nations.

Notes: Book reviews are solicited. Editorial reports on submissions in 30 to 60 days.

STUDIES ON THE DEVELOPING COUNTRIES

Executive editor: Leszek Cyrzyk

Editor-in-chief: Jerzy Prokopczuk

Editorial address:
>Polish Institute of International Affairs
>1a, Warecka Street
>P.O. Box 1000
>Warsaw, Poland

Sponsor: same as above

Frequency: SA   Founded: 1972
Subscription: 70 zlotys in Poland; $5 in
>U.S. and Canada; $4 other countries

Editorial interest:
>Chronological: 1945 to the present; current events
>Geographical: Africa, Asia, Latin America, West Indies, Middle East
>Topical: unrestricted, as long as it pertains to the special situation of developing countries

Editorial policies:
>Preferred length of ms.: approximately 36 typed pages
>Bottom notes. Preference given to Polish authors. Publishes in English.

Notes:
>Special feature: "Notes and News." Contains numerous book reviews and also "Shorter Notices" on books. Book reviews average four to five typed pages.

SUDAN JOURNAL OF ADMINISTRATION AND DEVELOPMENT

Editor: Osman Kheiri

Editorial address:
P.O. Box 1492
Khartoum, Democratic Republic of the Sudan

Sponsor: Institute of Public Administration

Frequency: A   Founded: 1965
Subscription: $3/£1

Editorial interest:
Chronological: current events
Geographical: Africa, Asia, Middle East
Topical: agriculture, anthropology, business, communications media,
cultural affairs, demography, economics, education, ethnology,
international organizations, legal and constitutional affairs,
politics and government, research methods, science and technology,
social history, transportation
Special scope: public administration, economic and social development
in developing nations

Editorial policies:
Query prior to submission of ms. preferred, but not necessary
Style manual: own house style, consult previous issues
Preferred length of ms.: 3,000-4,000 words; serialization considered
Author payment: 10 Sudanese pounds or equivalent, and 10 article
reprints
End notes. Accepts mss. and publishes articles in Arabic or English.
Articles should be directed to public service employees engaged in
economic and social development of emerging nations and to
students and researchers in this field. Wants articles that deal with
problems of public administration and reform, development administration, planning and plan execution, economics, sociological
and anthropological problems of social change and social adjust-
ment; most aspects of rapid social change.

Notes: Indexed in SSHI. Freelance book reviews from specialists are welcome;
remuneration same as for articles.

SURVEY OF RACE RELATIONS IN SOUTH AFRICA

Editor: R. M. de Villiers

Editorial address:
South African Institute of Race Relations
P.O. Box 97
Johannesburg, South Africa

Sponsor: same as above

Frequency: A   Founded: 1946
Subscription: $2.82/Rds 2 plus postage   Subscribers: 5,500

SURVEY OF RACE RELATIONS IN SOUTH AFRICA (cont'd)

Editorial interest:
>   Chronological: current events
>   Geographical: South Africa
>   Topical: sociology
>   Special scope: race relations

Editorial policies:
>   Staff-written and compiled. Published in English. "Presents latest statistics and estimates of population, cost of living, minimum income, education, legislation, economic situation as regards to the different groups, wages, taxes, pension, etc."

TANZANIA NOTES AND RECORDS: The Journal of the Tanzania Society

Editor: J. E. G. Sutton

Editorial address:
>   Tanzanian Society
>   P.O. Box 511
>   Dar es Salaam, Tanzania

Sponsor: same as above

Frequency: SA

Subscription: 30 Tanzanian shillings/$5/ £1.90

Founded: 1936 (as *Tanganyika Notes and Records*)

Subscribers: 1,200

Editorial interest:
>   Chronological: unrestricted
>   Geographical: Tanzania
>   Topical: unrestricted
>   Special scope: East Africa if related to Tanzania

Editorial policies:
>   Style manual: consult recent issues
>   Preferred length of ms.: open, depends on merit; no serialization
>   Author payment: 25 article reprints, more at cost to author if ordered in advance
>   Bottom notes. Accepts mss. and publishes articles in English and occasionally Swahili. Potential authors should write for an international, university-level audience interested in Tanzania. Wants mss. on anthropology, pre-history, history, geography, natural history, and related subjects. Articles should be well written but not overly specialized.

Notes: Articles abstracted or indexed in *Africa*, *African Abstracts*, HA
>   Special feature: "Current Bibliography of Tanzania." Book reviews are assigned, but freelance offerings might be considered if related to Tanzania; no remuneration. Editorial reports on submissions in two to four months.

TANZANIA ZAMANI: A Bulletin of Historical Research and Writing

Editor: J. E. G. Sutton

Editorial address:
> History Department
> University of Dar es Salaam
> P.O. Box 35050
> Dar es Salaam, Tanzania

Sponsors: Historical Association of Tanzania and University of Dar es Salaam

Frequency: SA

Subscription: 35s/$7

Founded: 1967

Subscribers: approximately 300

Editorial interest:
> Chronological: unrestricted
> Geographical: East Africa, Tanzania
> Topical: archaeology, discovery and exploration, historiography, social history
> Special scope: oral history and tradition of East Africa

Editorial policies:
> Query prior to submission of ms.
> Style manual: none prescribed
> Preferred length of ms.: 350-500 words; no serialization
> Author payment: none

Notes: An information sheet
> Special features: "Research by the History Department, University of Dar es Salaam," "Archaeological Research."

TARIKH

Editors: Obaro Ikime and Segun Osoba

Editorial address:
> Humanities Press, Inc.
> 303 Park Avenue South
> New York, New York 10010

Sponsor: Historical Society of Nigeria

Frequency: SA

Subscription: 36s/$5 for 2 years

Founded: 1965

Editorial interest:
> Chronological: unrestricted
> Geographical: Africa
> Topical: unrestricted
> Special scope: history

Editorial policies:
> Query prior to submission recommended, since each issue deals with a specific topic. Consult journal for style. Preference given to history professors at African universities.

TARIKH (cont'd)

Preferred length of ms.: 15 to 20 typed pages

"New syllabuses in African history are now in use or in preparation all over Africa though much of the most recent historical research in Africa is only available in advanced and expensive texts or in minds of scholars. *Tarikh* is an attempt to present some of this material in a readable and easily understood form for school and higher certificate and first year university students."

Notes: No book reviews

THEORIA: A Journal of Studies in the Arts, Humanities and Social Sciences

Editors: C. de B. Webb and E. H. Paterson

Editorial address:
P.O. Box 375
Pietermaritzburg, South Africa

Sponsor: University of Natal

Frequency: SA   Founded: 1947
Subscription: Rds 1   Subscribers: 300

Editorial interest:
Chronological: unrestricted
Geographical: worldwide
Topical: unrestricted

Editorial policies:
Query prior to submission of ms.
Style manual: none prescribed
Preferred length of ms.: 20 typed pages; serialization occasionally considered
Author payment: 10 article reprints and six copies of issue in which article appears
End notes. Accepts mss. and publishes in Afrikaans, English, French, or German. Most articles are in English. Address mss. to "The Editors" (names of the editors are not to be mentioned). Wants articles that appeal to academic readers with an interest in the humanities.

Notes: No book reviews. Editorial decisions on submissions shortly before March 15 and August 15; if offerings arrive after these dates, a potential author might have to wait several months for a report.

THOUGHT—NEW SERIES: A Journal of Afrikaans and English Thinking in South Africa

Editor: L. Holtz

Editorial address:
> South African Institute of Race Relations
> P.O. Box 97
> Johannesburg, South Africa

Sponsor: same as above

Frequency: Q   Founded: 1955
Subscription: $2.82/Rds 2 plus postage   Subscribers: 150

Editorial interest:
> Chronological: current events
> Geographical: South Africa
> Topical: economics, foreign relations, philosophy, social history
> Special scope: aparthied, Bantustans, inter-race relations

Editorial policies:
> Staff-written. A survey of editorial opinion in the Afrikaans and English press in South Africa. Published in English.

TRANSACTIONS OF THE HISTORICAL SOCIETY OF GHANA

Editor: J. O. Hunwick

Editorial address:
> Department of History
> University of Ghana
> P.O. Box 12
> Legon, Ghana

Frequency: A   Founded: 1950
Subscription: Cedi 1.50

Editorial interest:
> Chronological: unrestricted
> Geographical: Africa, Ghana, West Africa
> Topical: archaeology, auxiliary historical disciplines, discovery and exploration, historiography, social history
> Special scope: all aspects of Ghanaian and West African history

Editorial policies:
> Style manual: Hart's *Rules for Compositors and Printers*, 37th ed.; "Notes on Preparation of Mss." available on request
> Preferred length of ms.: around 8,000 words; longer articles accepted for serialization
> Author payment: 20 article reprints
> End notes. Accepts mss. and publishes articles in English. Potential authors should write for an audience of university readers and researchers, upper division college history teachers, and university students. Wants mss. incorporating new research into or new

TRANSACTIONS OF THE HISTORICAL SOCIETY OF
GHANA (cont'd)

interpretations of West African history. Research notes and communications welcome, including short English translations with commentary on historical source materials in little-known languages relating to Ghanaian and West African history.

Notes: Articles abstracted or cited in *African Abstracts*, HA, "Quarterly Bibliography" of *Africa*. Book reviews are solicited, but freelance review offerings will be considered; no remuneration.

TRANSITION

Editor: Rajat Neogy

Editorial address:
Box 9063
Accra, Ghana

Sponsors: Transition, Ltd., in association with the International Association for Cultural Freedom, Paris, France

Frequency: BM   Founded: 1961
Subscription: $7.10   Subscribers: 20,000

Editorial interest:
Chronological: unrestricted
Geographical: worldwide (African and Black emphasis)
Topical: anthropology, art, cultural affairs, economics, ethnology, politics and government

Editorial policies:
Query and abstract prior to submission of ms.
Preferred length of ms.: 2,000-10,000 words; accepts longer articles for serialization
Author payment: $100 or more and two copies of issue in which article appears
End notes. Accepts mss. and publishes articles in English. Interested in critical articles of African relevance but not necessarily confined to African issues alone.

Notes:
Special features: literary interviews, short stories, and poetry from both new and established writers. Book reviews are normally assigned. Reports on submissions in three to five months.

TROPICAL WORLD REVIEW

Editorial address:
Royal Tropical Institute
Mauritshade 63
Amsterdam, The Netherlands

TROPICAL WORLD REVIEW (cont'd)

Sponsor: same as above

Frequency: BM   Founded: 1971
Subscription: unreported

Editorial interest:
> Chronological: current events
> Geographical: Africa, Asia, Latin America, Middle East, West Indies
> Topical: agriculture, anthropology, bibliographical articles, business, church or ecclesiastical affairs, communications media, demography, economics, education, geography, politics and government, social history, sociology
> Special scope: economic geography, socio-economic developments in tropical areas

Editorial policies:
> Authors must be members of the Institute. No outside mss. will be accepted. Each issue is devoted to the economic geography of a single country and is introduced by a survey of that country's physical geography, history, and politics.

TWO TONE

Managing editor: Olive H. Robertson

Editorial address:
> 5 St. Breock Close
> Mount Pleasant, Salisbury, Rhodesia

Frequency: Q   Founded: 1965
Subscription: $1.25

Editorial interest:
> Chronological: unrestricted
> Geographical: Africa, Rhodesia
> Topical: literature (history and criticism)
> Special scope: indigenous poetry and its development

Editorial policies:
> Query prior to submission of ms. optional
> Style manual: none prescribed
> Preferred length of ms.: poems of not more than 40 lines
> Author payment: three copies of issue in which poem appears
> Bottom notes. Accepts mss. and publishes poetry in English, Shona, or Sindebele. Wants short verse, mainly lyrical, and mss. dealing with indigenous verse and its development. The managing editor is prepared to publish poems occasionally from other countries.

Notes: Poems and articles are cited in *Rhodesian Archives*. Book reviews are assigned; no remuneration. Persons interested in reviewing should contact the managing editor. Since the editorship revolves for each issue, submissions are retained for a year so each of the four consecutive editors can consider the mss.; if they have not been published after a year, they are withdrawn.

UFAHAMU

Editor: Teshombe Gabriel

Editorial address:
  African Studies Center
  University of California
  Los Angeles, California 90024

Sponsor: African Activist Association

Frequency: TA

Subscription: $4 individual in U.S.; $5
  elsewhere; $10 institutional

Founded: 1970

Subscribers: approximately
  400

Editorial interest:
  Chronological: unrestricted
  Geographical: Africa, United States
  Topical: anthropology, art, auxiliary historical disciplines, bibliographi-
    cal articles, cinema and film, communications media, cultural
    affairs, economics, education, ethnology, folklore, foreign rela-
    tions, geography, historiography, history of ideas, language (phi-
    ology, semantics), literature (history and criticism), military
    affairs, politics and government, religious studies, social history,
    sociology, theatre and drama
  Special scope: African liberation movements, Third World studies,
    United States business investment in Africa

Editorial policies:
  Query prior to submission of ms.
  Style manual: none prescribed, consult previous issues
  Preferred length of ms.: 15-20 *Ufahamu* pages (45 lines per page);
    serialization rare
  Author payment: two to five copies of issue in which article appears
  End notes. Accepts mss. and publishes articles in English. Authors
    should write for an audience interested in Afro-American and
    African questions and topics. Articles should challenge established
    theses and assumptions about Africa, should tend to create con-
    troversy or reflect radical perspectives, and should cover contem-
    porary events in Africa, especially liberation movements. *Ufahamu*
    is published by graduate students at the University of California,
    Los Angeles. Contributions by students are especially welcomed:
    well over half of the articles published are by students. "We serve
    as a forum for new perspectives on Africa, to provoke reevaluations
    of established assumptions, to serve as a catalyst for stimulating
    new debates on Africa's past, present, and future, and, above all, to
    give voice to the aspirations of African liberation struggles."

Notes: Articles abstracted or cited in *Radical Africana* (published by African
  Studies Center, Edinburgh University, Edinburgh, Scotland)
  Special features: bibliographies. Book reviews normally assigned, but
    freelance offerings welcomed; no remuneration. Reviews may be as
    long as five typed pages. Send reviews to book review editor. Re-
    ports on submissions in approximately two months.

UGANDA JOURNAL

Editor: B. W. Langlands

Editorial address:
P.O. Box 4980
Kampala, Uganda

Sponsor: The Uganda Society

Frequency: SA
Subscription: 60 Ugandan shillings/$9/
£3.15

Founded: 1934
Subscribers: 800

Editorial interest:
Chronological: unrestricted
Geographical: Uganda
Topical: agriculture, anthropology, archaeology, auxiliary historical
disciplines, bibliographical articles, church or ecclesiastical affairs,
cultural affairs, demography, discovery and exploration, education, ethnology, folklore, geography, historiography, history of
ideas, language (philology, semantics), medicine (history), military affairs, music (history), religious studies, sociology

Editorial policies:
Query prior to submission of ms. optional
Style manual: any
Preferred length of ms.: 10,000 words maximum; will consider longer
articles for serialization only in exceptional circumstances
Author payment: 20 article reprints
End notes. Accepts mss. and publishes articles in English. Potential
authors should write for an academic and university level audience.
Wants mss. relating to Uganda.

Notes: Articles abstracted in *African Abstracts*, HA
Special feature: bibliography on Uganda. Book reviews are usually
solicited, but will consider freelance offerings if work relates to
Uganda.

UMBRA

Editor: David Henderson

Editorial address:
Box 374
Peter Stuyvesant Station
New York, New York 10009

Frequency: TA
Subscription: $3 in U.S.; $4 elsewhere

Founded: 1961
Subscribers: 1,500

Editorial interest:
Chronological: unrestricted (mostly current events)
Geographical: Africa, United States, West Indies

UMBRA (cont'd)

> Topical: art, cinema and film, communications media, cultural affairs, education, ethnology, folklore, history of ideas, language (philology, semantics), literature (history and criticism), music (history), theatre and drama
>
> Special scope: Black literature and art, Black poetry

Editorial policies:

> Articles are usually solicited. Accepts mss. in English, French, or Spanish. Publishes in English (and occasionally Spanish).

Notes: Reports on unsolicited submissions in three to six months.

UNIVERSITAS

Editor: K. E. Senanu

Editorial address:

> Department of English
> University of Ghana
> P.O. Box 69
> Legon, Ghana

Sponsor: same as above

Frequency: SA

Subscription: Cedi 1.50

Founded: 1954

Subscribers: approximately 250

Editorial interest:

> Chronological: unrestricted
> Geographical: worldwide
> Topical: unrestricted

Editorial policies:

> Query prior to submission of ms.
> Style manual: any scholarly style
> Preferred length of ms.: unrestricted; accepts long articles
> Author payment: one copy of issue in which article appears and three article reprints
> End notes. Potential authors should write for a university-educated general public. Wants mss. on educational topics and of general interest.

Notes: Articles indexed in SSHI. Freelance book reviews are welcomed; no remuneration. Editorial reports on submissions as soon as possible.

UNIVERSITY OF GHANA LAW JOURNAL

Editors: G. R. Woodman, S. K. Date-Bah, and A. K. P. Sawyerr

Editorial address:

> Faculty of Law
> University of Ghana
> Legon, Ghana

UNIVERSITY OF GHANA LAW JOURNAL (cont'd)

Sonsor: same as above

Frequency: SA
Subscription: $15

Founded: 1964
Subscribers: 250

Editorial interest:
> Chronological: unrestricted
> Geographical: Africa
> Topical: legal and constitutional affairs

Editorial policies:
> Style manual: same as British legal periodicals
> Preferred length of ms.: 8,000 words; serialization accepted
> Author payment: 25 article reprints
> Bottom or end notes. Accepts mss. and publishes articles in English.
>> Mss. should be directed to an audience of lawyers interested in Africa.

Notes: Cited in *Index to Foreign Legal Periodicals*
> Special features: "Notes and Comments" dealing with restricted, typical subjects and particularly with recent developments in Ghanian law. Book reviews are solicited, but freelance offerings are considered. Persons interested in reviewing should write to the editors; no remuneration. Editorial decision on submissions normally within one month.

WEST AFRICA

Editor: David Morgan Williams

Editorial address:
> Cromwell House
> Fulwood Place
> London WC1, England

Frequency: W
Subscription: £7.80 in U.K.; $21 in U.S.

Founded: 1917
Subscribers: approximately 15,000

Editorial interest:
> Chronological: unrestricted
> Geographical: West Africa
> Topical: agriculture, anthropology, archaeology, architecture, art, auxiliary historical disciplines, business, communications media, discovery and exploration, economics, education, ethnology, folklore, foreign relations, frontier areas, geography, historiography, history of ideas, international organizations, language (philology, semantics), legal and constitutional affairs, literature (history and criticism), maritime history, medicine (history), military affairs, music (history), naval affairs, philosophy, philosophy of history, science and technology, social history, sociology, theatre and drama, transportation

WEST AFRICA (cont'd)

Editorial policies:
    Query prior to submission of ms.
    Style manual: none prescribed
    Preferred length of ms.: 800-1,200 words; longer articles accepted
        according to merit
    Author payment: arranged
    End notes

Notes: Book reviews "assigned by arrangement"

WEST AFRICAN JOURNAL OF ARCHAEOLOGY

Editor: Thurstan Shaw

Assistant editors: Graham Connah and Paul Dzanne

Editorial address:
    Institute of African Studies
    University of Ibadan
    Ibadan, Nigeria

Sponsors: University of Ibadan, University of Ife, University of Ghana, University College of Cape Coast, and Ghana Museum and Monuments Board

Frequency: A

Subscription: N₤2.26/Fr 33

Founded: 1964 (as *West African Archaeological Newsletter*; name changed in 1971)

Subscribers: approximately 500

Editorial interest:
    Chronological: pre-history to 1800
    Geographical: Africa, West Africa
    Topical: archaeology, research methods

Editorial policies:
    Query prior to submission of ms. optional
    Style manual: *Author's and Printer's Dictionary* (Oxford University Press); "Instructions to Contributors" printed in each issue
    Preferred length of ms.: 7,500-10,000 words; accepts longer articles for serialization
    Author payment: 25 article reprints
    Uses modified Harvard Style reference system; consult journal for specifications. Accepts mss. and publishes articles in English or French. Potential authors should write for an audience of professional archaeologists. Wants reports with illustrations, original fieldwork and excavation, and mss. on archaeological methodology, and of synthesis.

Notes:
    Special feature: field reports of original work in African archaeology, especially West Africa. Potential contributors should submit the

original and one copy of the ms., typed, double-spaced on quarto paper, along with a 120- to 300-word summary. Refer to K. K. Landis, "A Scrutiny of the Abstract," *Bull. Am. Assoc. Petrol. Geol.* 50:9 (1966) 1992, for style and content of summary. Book reviews are assigned and solicited, but freelance offerings are considered; no remuneration.

WEST AFRICAN JOURNAL OF EDUCATION

Editors: J. A. Majasan and E. A. Yoloye

Assistant editor: J. O. O. Abiri

Editorial address:
Institute of Education
University of Ibadan
Ibadan, Nigeria

Sponsor: same as above

Frequency: TA
Subscription: $7

Founded: 1957
Subscribers: 700
Circulation: 1,500

Editorial interest:
Chronological: unrestricted
Geographical: Africa
Topical: education
Special scope: research and innovations in education

Editorial policies:
Style manual: none prescribed
Preferred length of ms.: 1,500-3,000 words; serialization occasionally considered
Author payment: none, but article reprints can be ordered in advance at a nominal charge
Bottom notes. Accepts mss. and publishes articles in English or French. Potential authors should write for an audience of teachers, teacher-trainees and anyone interested in West Africa in particular and Africa in general. Articles should pertain to education in West Africa or be relevant to it.

Notes:
Special features: some issues are dedicated to a single topic, such as "Organization of Education in Africa" (February 1972), "Education and Employment in Africa" (February 1973). Potential authors should submit two copies of ms. typed double-spaced on quarto size paper. Book reviews are assigned, but freelance offerings would be considered if the book reviewed was available in West Africa or was relevant to education in West Africa. Persons interested in reviewing should contact the editors. Editorial reports on submissions in two to three months.

WIENER VOLKERKUNDLICHE MITTEILUNGEN

Editorial address:
Osterreichische Ethnologische Gesellschaft
Museum für Voelkerkunde
A-1014 Vienna
Neue Hofburg, Austria

Sponsor: same as above

Frequency: A
Subscription: S 71

Founded: 1952
Subscribers: 750

Editorial interest:
Chronological: unspecified
Geographical: Africa, Asia, Canada, Latin America, Middle East, United
States, West Indies
Topical: anthropology, discovery and exploration, ethnology, folklore,
religious studies, research methods, social history

Editorial policies:
Query prior to submission of ms. optional
Style manual: none prescribed
Preferred length of ms.: 20 typed pages; longer articles accepted for
serialization
Author payment: 20 article reprints
End notes. Accepts mss. and publishes articles in English, German, or
Spanish.

Notes:
Special features: a full list of anthropological lectures and doctoral
theses at Vienna University; news of current field work. No book
reviews. Editorial reports on submissions in approximately two
months.

WINGS OVER AFRICA

Editor: J. K. Chilwell

Editorial address:
Aviation Publications Proprietary, Ltd.
Box 68585
82 Culross Road
Bryanston, Transvaal, South Africa

Frequency: M
Subscription: $9/Rds 4.80

Founded: 1941
Circulation: 10,000

Editorial interest:
Chronological: current events
Geographical: Africa
Topical: air forces
Special scope: aviation in all its aspects as related to Africa

WINGS OVER AFRICA (cont'd)

Editorial policies:
> Query prior to submission of ms.
> Style manual: none prescribed
> Preferred length of ms.: not reported
> Author payment: Rds 15 per printed page minimum, and one copy of the issue in which article appears
> Bottom notes. Accepts mss. and publishes articles in English. Potential authors should write for an audience interested in aviation.

Notes: Freelance book review offerings are welcome if the material relates to aviation in Africa. Editorial reports on submissions within one month.

WORLD OF ISLAM / MONDE DE L'ISLAM / WELT DES ISLAMS

Editor: Otto Spies

Editorial address:
> Orientalisches Seminar der Universität Bonn
> Liefrauenweg 7
> Bonn/Rhein, Federal Republic of Germany

Frequency: A (in two parts)　　　　Founded: 1910
Subscription: DM 32　　　　　　　Subscribers: approximately
　　　　　　　　　　　　　　　　　　　　300

Editorial interest:
> Chronological: 1600 to present
> Geographical: Africa, Asia, Middle East (mostly)
> Topical: bibliographical articles, cultural affairs, language (philology), literature (history and criticism), politics and government, religious studies
> Special scope: Oriental languages, literature, politics

Editorial policies:
> Query prior to submission of ms.
> Style manual: none
> Preferred length of ms.: 10-60 typed pages; no serialization
> Author payment: 20 article reprints
> Bottom or end notes. Accepts mss. and publishes articles in English, French, or German. Wants mss. that deal with the historical development of Islam, contemporary political and religious Islamic ideas, contemporary history of Islamic states.

Notes: Articles cited in *Bibliography of Islamic Peoples, Literature, Culture and Religion*. All mss. must be ready for the press; any alterations by the author after acceptance will be charged to the author. Book reviews are assigned and solicited, but freelance offerings are considered; no remuneration. Persons interested in reviewing should contact the editor. Editorial reports on submissions in two to three weeks.

ZAMBEZIA: A Journal of Southern and Central Africa

Editor: R. S. Roberts

Editorial address:
> University of Rhodesia
> P.O. Box M.P. 167
> Salisbury, Rhodesia

Sponsor: same as above

Frequency: A   Founded: 1967
Subscription: Rhodesian pounds 1   Subscribers: 300

Editorial interest:
> Chronological: unrestricted
> Geographical: Central and Southern Africa
> Topical: agriculture, anthropology, archaeology, architecture, art, auxiliary historical disciplines, bibliographical articles, business, church or ecclesiastical affairs, communications media, cultural affairs, discovery and exploration, economics, education, ethnology, folklore, foreign relations, frontier areas, geography, historiography, language (philology, semantics), legal and constitutional affairs, literature (history and criticism), maritime history, medicine (history), politics and government, religious studies, research methods, theatre and drama, transportation

Editorial policies:
> Style manual: "Notes to Contributors" available on request
> Preferred length of ms.: 6,000 words; accepts longer articles for serialization; short research reports of 500-1,000 words welcomed
> Author payment: 10 article reprints
> Bottom or end notes. Accepts mss. and publishes articles in English.

Notes: Potential authors should submit original and one copy of ms. Margins of 1 inch to 1½ inch on both sides of paper. Freelance book reviews of 500-1,000 words are welcomed.

ZAMBIA MUSEUMS JOURNAL

Editors: Kafungulwa Mubitana and L. Holy

Editorial address:
> Livingstone Museum
> P.O. Box 498
> Livingstone, Zambia

Sponsor: National Museums Board of Zambia, P.O. Box 198, Lusaka, Zambia

Frequency: A   Founded: 1970
Subscription: Zambian pounds 1.20/$1.68/
> £.70

Editorial interest:
> Chronological: unrestricted

ZAMBIA MUSEUMS JOURNAL (cont'd)

Geographical: Africa, Zambia
Topical: anthropology, art, cultural affairs, ethnology, folklore,
    research methods, social history, sociology

Editorial policies:
Query prior to submission of ms.
Style manual: none prescribed
Preferred length of ms.: 5,000 words; no serialization
Author payment: 25-50 article reprints
Bottom or end notes. Accepts mss. and publishes articles in English.
    Potential authors should write for an academic or general audience.
    Wants mss. that deal with developing nations and that have some
    relation to Zambia.

Notes: Freelance book reviews are welcomed. Persons interested in reviewing
    should write the editors. Editorial reports on submissions within three
    months.

ZAMBIAN LAW JOURNAL

Editor-in-chief: R. B. Kent

Associate editors: M. R. Zafer and C. P. Gupta

Editorial address:
School of Law
P.O. Box 2379
Lusaka, Zambia

Sponsor: University of Zambia

Frequency: SA   Founded: 1969
Subscription: $6.25   Subscribers: 188

Editorial interest:
Chronological: unrestricted
Geographical: Africa, Zambia
Topical: economics, foreign relations, frontier areas, international law,
    international organizations, legal and constitutional affairs,
    politics and government

Editorial policies:
Style manual: any
Preferred length of ms.: 30 typed pages; serialization acceptable
Author payment: 30 article reprints
Bottom notes. Accepts mss. and publishes articles in English. Potential
    authors should write for an audience of lawyers and others inter-
    ested in law development in Africa, particularly Zambia. Wants
    mss. relating to legal and economic development and political
    and social change.

Notes: Freelance book reviews welcomed; no remuneration. Editorial reports
    on submissions in about two months.

ZAMBIAN REVIEW

Editor: Allan G. Smith

Editorial address:
P.O. Box 717
Ndola, Zambia

Sponsor: Associated Reviews, Ltd.

Frequency: M
Subscription: $2.07/3 Zambian pounds

Founded: 1963
Subscribers: approximately
3,000

Editorial interest:
Chronological: current events
Geographical: Zambia
Topical: unrestricted

Editorial policies:
Query prior to submission of ms.
Style manual: none prescribed
Preferred length of ms.: not reported
Accepts mss. and publishes in English. No further information reported.

ZAMBIAN URBAN STUDIES

Editor: S. Nieuwolt

Editorial address:
Department of Geography
University of Zambia
P.O. Box 2379
Lusaka, Zambia

Sponsor: Institute of Social Research, University of Zambia

Frequency: irr., but at least one issue
per year
Subscription: $1 per issue

Founded: 1969
Subscribers: approximately
450

Editorial interest:
Chronological: unrestricted
Geographical: Africa, Zambia
Topical: geography, social history, sociology
Special scope: urban geography, urban sociology

Editorial policies:
Style manual: none prescribed
Preferred length of ms.: unrestricted, but generally not more than 50
typed pages; no serialization
Author payment: 20 article reprints
End notes. Accepts mss. and publishes articles in English. Potential
authors should write for an audience of Zambian intellectuals,
geographers, and sociologists. Wants mss. on urban geography and
urban sociology relating to Zambian conditions.

ZAMBIAN URBAN STUDIES (cont'd)

Notes:
>
> Special features: maps and diagrams. No book reviews. Editorial reports on submissions in one month.

ZIMBABWE NEWS

Editorial address:
> P.O. Box 2331
> Lusaka, Zambia

Sponsor: Zimbabwe African National Union (ZANU)

Frequency: M	Founded: 1965
Subscription: $10	Subscribers: 3,500

Editorial interest:
> Chronological: unrestricted (main emphasis on nineteenth century to
> the present)
> Geographical: Africa
> Topical: politics and government

Editorial policies:
> Preferred length of ms.: approximately 600-1,000 words; articles are
> accepted for serialization, but they must be short (approximately
> 1,000 words)
> Author payment: none
> Bottom notes. Would like to see political articles in the anti-imperialist,
> anti-colonial, and anti-neo-colonial struggle.

Notes:
> Special features: sections on the anti-imperialist struggles, British
> colonial history in Southern Africa, and South African and
> Portuguese colonial and imperialist attitudes and history.

ADDENDA

Despite the best efforts of the compilers, some periodicals did not respond to questionnaires. For the user's convenience these periodicals are listed here in alphabetical order; prospective authors are encouraged to write to the editors to secure information concerning the editorial scope of interest and editorial policies.

Abbia (Cameroon)
Africa (Johannesburg)
Africa and the World (London)
Africa-Kenkyu (Tokyo)
Africa Quarterly (New Delhi)
Africa South of the Sahara (London)
African Historian (Nigeria)
African Language Review (Sierra Leone)
Africana (Nairobi)
Afro-Asian and World Affairs (New Delhi)
Afro-Asian Bulletin (Cairo)
Afro-Asian Peoples (Cairo)
Afroculture (Nigeria)
Bushara (Nairobi)
Black Dialogue (New York)
Black Expressions (Chicago)
Black Position (Detroit)
Commando (Pretoria)
East African Linguistic Studies (Uganda)
Education in Eastern Africa (Nairobi)
1860 Settler, The (Durban)
Entente Africaine (Paris)
Ghala (Nairobi)
Journal of African Law (London)
Journal of Islamic Studies (Cairo)
Journal of the Historical Society of Nigeria (Nigeria)
Journal of the Language Association of East Africa (Nairobi)
Kush (Khartoum)
Lantern (Pretoria)
Liberator (New York)

ADDENDA (cont'd)

Liberian Historical Review (Liberia)
Liberian Law Journal (Liberia)
Nigerian Geographical Journal (Nigeria)
Nigerian Journal of Economic and Social Studies (Nigeria)
Optima (Johannesburg)
Quarterly Review of Higher Education Among Negroes
  (North Carolina)
Race Today (London)
Sierra Leone Bulletin of Religion (Sierra Leone)
Sierra Leone Geographical Journal (Sierra Leone)
Somaliland Journal (Somaliland)
South African Journal of Economics (Johannesburg)
Spekulum (Pretoria)
Studies in African History, Anthropology and Ethnology
  (The Hague)
Sudan Notes and Records (Khartoum)
Swaziland Annual (Johannesburg)
Transafrican Journal of History (Nairobi)
University (Zambia)

ANALYTICAL INDEX

The Analytical Index is divided into four major categories. The first category, General—Unrestricted, lists those periodicals reporting no limitations on any of the three aspects of their editorial scope of interest (chronological, geographical, or topical). The periodicals included in this category are not listed in any of the other three categories of the index. The Chronological, Geographical, and Topical divisions of the index are first subdivided by the term "Unrestricted," which denotes periodicals with a wide field of interest. An asterisk (*) signifies that special attention should be given to the remarks made in the main entry that may modify the journal's scope of interest. The periodicals reporting no restrictions upon a particular category are listed under "Unspecified" at the end of each index.

GENERAL—UNRESTRICTED

Drum *
Theoria
Universitas

CHRONOLOGICAL INDEX

Unrestricted

Journals listed here indicated no limitations on periods or years of interest. See also the index General—Unrestricted.

Aberdeen University African Studies
  Group Bulletin
AFER
Africa
Africa Report
African Arts
African Challenge *

African Language Studies
African Literature Today
African Music *
African Notes
African Progress
African Quarterly
African Research and Documentation *

Pre-History to the Nineteenth Century

1000 B.C. to the Nineteenth Century

410 to 1492

500 to 1500

622 to the Present

Islam

1100 to the Present

Ethiopian Observer
Studia Musicologia

1600 to the Present

Asian and African Studies
Kroniek van Afrika

National Scene Magazine Supplement
World of Islam

Nineteenth Century to the Present

Assegai

1900 to the Present

Africa Today
African Affairs
African Communist
Afrika Spectrum
Eastern Africa Economic Review
Institute of Development Studies
  Bulletin*

Journal of Commonwealth and
  Comparative Politics
Lotus
Pan-African Journal
Rhodesian Journal of Economics
Round Table
Springbok

1945 to the Present

Studies on the Developing
  Countries

Current Events

Africa Institute Bulletin
Africa Magazine
Africa Research Bulletin
African Affairs
African Communist
African Development

African Law Digest
African Law Studies
Agricultural Economics Bulletin for
  Africa
Annual Report of the South African
  Institute of Race Relations

Asia and Africa Review
Asian and African Studies
Assegai
Black Arts Magazine
Black Enterprise
Black Theatre
Correspondance d'Orient Etudes
Daily News-Sunday News*
East African Agricultural and
  Forestry Journal
Eastern Africa Economic Review
Ethiopian Observer
Forum (University of Ghana)
Ghana Journal of Education
Howard Law Journal*
Journal of Commonwealth and
  Comparative Politics
Kroniek van Afrika
Legon Observer
Manpower and Unemployment
  Research in Africa

Negro American Literature Forum
Negro Educational Review
Okike
Pan-African Journal
Review of Black Political Economy
Rhodesia Agricultural Journal
Rhodesia and World Report
Rhodesian Journal of Economics
Sepia Magazine
South African Law Journal
Spear
Studies on the Developing Countries
Sudan Journal of Administration and
  Development
Survey of Race Relations in South
  Africa
Thought—New Series
Tropical World Review
Wings Over Africa
Zambian Review

GEOGRAPHICAL INDEX

Worldwide

Journals listed here indicated no restrictions on geographical areas of interest. See also the index General—Unrestricted.

African Challenge*
Assegai
Beau-Cocoa
Civilisations*
Comparative and International Law
  Journal of Southern Africa*
Daily News-Sunday News
Eastern Africa Law Review
Focus
Institute of Development Studies
  Bulletin*
Journal of Developing Areas

Journal of Development Studies
Journal of Negro History
Kleio
Mankind Quarterly
Military History Journal*
Negro History Bulletin*
Okike
Phylon
Race
Second Order
Transition

Africa

Asia

*American Portuguese Cultural Society Journal**
Archiv Orientálni
Asia and Africa Review
Asian and African Studies
Bulletin: British Association of Orientalists
Bulletin de la Société de Géographie d'Egypte
Correspondance d'Orient Etudes
Development and Change
*East Africa Journal**
Ethnos
Folia Orientalia
Freedomways
Islam
Journal of Asian and African Studies
Journal of Commonwealth Literature
Journal of Commonwealth and Comparative Politics
Journal of Topical Geography
*Lotus**
Manpower and Unemployment Research in Africa
Le Muséon
Muslim World
Overseas Development
Rocznik Orientalistyczny
Round Table
School of Oriental and African Studies Bulletin
Studia Musicologia
Studia Orientalia
Studies on Developing Countries
Studies on the Developing Countries
*Sudan Journal of Administration and Development**
Tropical World Review
Wiener Volkerkundliche Mitteilungen
World of Islam

Australia

Ethnos
Journal of Commonwealth Literature

Balkans

Islam
Studia Musicologia

Brazil

American Portuguese Cultural Society Journal

British Commonwealth

Round Table

Canada

African Progress*
Black Academy Review*
Black Creation
Black Enterprise
Crisis*
Freedomways
Harvard Journal of Afro-American
  Affairs*

Journal of Commonwealth Literature
Journal of Commonwealth and
  Comparative Politics
Overseas Development
Presence Africaine*
Round Table
Wiener Volkerkundliche Mitteilungen

Central Africa

African Social Research*
Nada
Zambezia

East Africa

Bulletin: British Association of
  Orientalists
East African Geographical Review*

Eastern Africa Economic Review
Tanzia Zamani

Eastern Europe

African Communist*
Archiv Orientálni
Freedomways
Lotus*

Rocznik Orientalistyczny
Speculum
Studia Musicologia

Ethiopia

Ethiopian Geographical Journal
Ethiopian Observer

Journal of Ethiopian Law
Journal of Ethiopian Studies

Far East

Rocznik Orientalistyczny

Ghana

*Transactions of the Historical Society
of Ghana*

Iberia

Islam

Latin America

Africa Magazine*
African Notes
Afro-American Studies
Black Academy Review*
Black Arts Magazine
Black Theatre
Black World*
*Current Bibliography on
African Affairs*
Development and Change
East Africa Journal*
Essence
Ethnos
Forum, The
Freedomways
*Harvard Journal of Afro-
American Affairs**

Journal of Black Studies
Journal of Tropical Geography
Lotus*
*Manpower and Unemployment Research
in Africa*
National Scene Magazine Supplement*
Overseas Development
Pan-African Journal
Round Table
Sepia Magazine
Studies on Developing Countries
Studies on the Developing Countries
Tropical World Review
Wiener Volkerkundliche Mitteilungen

Liberia

Liberian Studies Journal

Malawi

Society of Malawi Journal

Mediterranean

Le Muséon

Russia/USSR

Archiv Orientálni
Bulletin: British Association of
 Orientalists
Freedomways
Islam*

Lotus*
Muslim World*
Rocznik Orientalistyczny
Speculum
Studia Musicologia

Scandinavia

Speculum

Sierra Leone

Africana Research Bulletin
Sierra Leone Studies

South Africa

Annual Report of the South
 African Institute of Race
 Relations
Nada
Race Relations News

South African Law Journal
Survey of Race Relations in South
 Africa
Thought–New Series

South America

Review of Black Political
 Economy*

Southern Africa

Rhodesia Agricultural Journal
Rhodesia and World Report
Zambezia

Tanzania

Tanzania Notes and Records*
Tanzania Zamani

GEOGRAPHICAL INDEX (cont'd)

Uganda

Uganda Journal

USSR—*See* Russia

United Kingdon

Journal of Administration Overseas

United States

Africa Magazine *
African Notes
African Communist *
African Progress *
Afro-American Studies
Black Academy Review *
Black Arts Magazine
Black Creation
Black Enterprise
Black Scholar *
Black Theatre
Black World *
Cricket
Crisis *
Current Bibliography on African Affairs *
Essence
Forum, The
Freedomways
Harvard Journal of Afro-American Affairs *
Howard Law Journal
Journal of Black Studies
Journal of Negro Education
Journal of the New African Literature and the Arts
National Scene Magazine Supplement *
Negro American Literature Forum
Overseas Development
Negro Educational Review
Pan-African Journal
Presence Africaine *
Renaissance 2
Review of Black Political Economy
Round Table
Sepia Magazine
Studies in Black Literature
Studies in Race and Nations
Ufahamu *
Umbra
Wiener Volkerkundliche Mitteilungen

West Africa

Odu
Sierra Leone Studies
Transactions of the Historical Society of Ghana

West Africa
West African Journal of Archaeology

West Indies

Western Europe

Zambia

TOPICAL INDEX

Unrestricted

Journals listed here indicated no restrictions on subject matter. See also the index General—Unrestricted.

Aberdeen University African Studies Group Bulletin
Africa Report
Africa Research Bulletin
African Quarterly
African Research and Documentation
African Social Research *
Africana Bulletin
Africana News and Notes *
American Portuguese Cultural Society Journal *
Black Scholar *
Canadian Journal of African Studies
Current Bibliography on African Affairs *
Development and Change
Essence *

Focus
Forum (University of Ghana)
Harvard Journal of Afro-American Affairs *
Ibadan *
Insight and Opinion
Liberian Studies Journal
Munger Africana Library Notes
Negro History Bulletin
Newsletter of the Western Association of Africanists
Odu
Papers in International Studies
Sierra Leone Studies
Spear
Studies on the Developing Countries *
Tanzania Notes and Records
Tarikh
Zambian Review

Agriculture

Africa Institute Bulletin
Africa Magazine
African Challenge
African Development
African Notes
African Progress
African Studies Review
Afrika Spectrum
Africultural Economics Bulletin for Africa
Bulletin de la Société de Géographie d'Egypte
Cahiers d'Etudes Africaines
Civilisations *
Daily News-Sunday News
East African Agricultural and Forestry Journal *
East African Geographical Review

Ethiopian Geographical Journal
Ethiopian Observer
Journal of Developing Areas *
Journal of Tropical Geography
Legon Observer
Manpower and Unemployment Research in Africa
Overseas Development
Pan-African Journal
Presence Africaine
Review of Black Political Economy
Rhodesia Agricultural Journal
Rhodesian Journal of Economics
Round Table
Rural Africana
School of Oriental and African Studies Bulletin
Society of Malawi Journal

180

South African Geographical
 Journal*
Studies on Developing Countries*
Sudan Journal of Administration
 and Development

Tropical World Review
Uganda Journal
West Africa
Zambezia

Air Forces

See also Military Affairs and Naval Affairs.

Assegai
Military History Journal
Round Table

Société des Africanistes Journal
Springbok*
Wings Over Africa*

Anthropology

AFER
Africa
Africa Institute Bulletin
African Affairs
African Notes
African Scholar
African Studies
African Studies Review
African Urban Notes
Africana Marburgensia
Africana Research Bulletin
Afrika Spectrum
Afro-American Studies
Archiv Orientálni
Asian and African Studies
Azania*
Ba Shiru
Black Academy Review*
Black Theatre
Black World
Bulletin: British Association of
 Orientalists
Bulletin de la Société de
 Géographie d'Egypte
Cahiers d'Etudes Africaines*
Conch
Crisis
East African Geographical Review

Ethiopian Geographical Journal
Ethiopian Observer
Ethnos
Folia Orientalia
Freedomways
Institute for the Study of Man in
 Africa*
Islam
Journal of Asian and African Studies
Journal of Black Studies
Journal of Ethiopian Studies
Journal of Negro History
Journal of Semitic Studies
Journal of the New African Literature
 and the Arts
Journal of the S.W.A. Scientific Society
Journal of Tropical Geography
Kleio
Kroniek van Afrika
Lotus
Manpower and Unemployment Research
 in Africa
Le Muséon
Nada*
Overseas Development
Pan-African Journal
Phylon*
Presence Africaine

Archaeology

Architecture

African Urban Notes
Antiquaries Journal
Archaeologia
Archiv Orientálni
Beau-Cocoa
Black Academy Review*
Black Theatre
Bulletin: British Association of
  Orientalists
Ethiopian Observer
Islam
Journal of Black Studies
Journal of Developing Areas*

Journal of Ethiopian Studies
Kleio
Lotus
Presence Africaine
Rural Africana
School of Oriental and African Studies
  Bulletin
Société des Africanistes Journal
Society of Malawi Journal
Speculum
West Africa
Zambezia

Art

AFER
Africa
Africa Today
African Arts*
African Music*
African Notes
African Progress
African Studies Review
Africana Research Bulletin
Afro-American Studies
Antiquaries Journal
Archaeologia
Archiv Orientálni
Asia and Africa Review
Asian and African Studies
Ba Shiru
Beau-Cocoa
Black Academy Review*
Black Art Magazine*
Black Creation
Black Theatre
Black World
Bulletin: British Association of
  Orientalists
Cahiers d'Etudes Africaines
Chronique d'Egypte
Conch
Cricket
Crisis

Ethiopian Observer
Ethnos
Folia Orientalia
Forum, The
Freedomways
Institute for the Study of Man in
  Africa*
Islam
Journal of Black Studies
Journal of Developing Areas*
Journal of Ethiopian Studies
Journal of Negro History
Lotus
Nada*
Negro American Literature Forum
Phylon*
Renaissance 2
Rocznik Orientalistyczny
Société des Africanistes Journal
Society of Malawi Journal
Speculum
Transition
Ufahamu
Umbra
West Africa
Zambezia
Zambia Museums Journal

Auxiliary Historical Disciplines

Bibliographical Articles

TOPICAL INDEX (cont'd)

Rural Africana
School of Oriental and African
  Studies Bulletin
Société des Africanistes Journal
Society of Malawi Journal
South West African Scientific
  Society Newsletter

Tropical World Review
Ufahamu
Uganda Journal
World of Islam*
Zambezia

Business

Africa Institute Bulletin
Africa Magazine
African Development
African Progress
African Studies Review
African Urban Notes
Afro-American Studies
Black Enterprise
Howard Law Journal
Institute of Development Studies
  Bulletin*
Journal of Business and Social
  Studies
Journal of Developing Areas*
Manpower and Unemployment
  Research in Africa

National Scene Magazine
  Supplement
Negro Educational Review
Review of Black Political Economy
Rhodesian Journal of Economics
Round Table
Rural Africana
Sepia Magazine
Society of Malawi Journal
Sudan Journal of Administration and
  Development
Tropical World Review
West Africa
Zambezia

Church or Ecclesiastical Affairs (denominational, institutional)

See also Religious Studies.

AFER
Africa Today
African Challenge
Africana Marburgensia
Africana Research Bulletin
Afrika Spectrum
Beau-Cocoa
Cahiers d'Etudes Africaines
Journal of Developing Areas*
Journal of Ethiopian Studies
Journal of Religion in Africa
Kleio

Le Muséon
Muslim World
National Scene Magazine Supplement
Presence Africaine
Review of Black Political Economy
Rural Africana
School of Oriental and African Studies
  Bulletin
Sepia Magazine
Tropical World Review
Uganda Journal
Zambezia

TOPICAL INDEX (cont'd)

Cinema and Film

See also Theatre and Drama.

African Arts*
Beau-Cocoa
Black Arts Magazine
Black Theatre
National Scene Magazine
  Supplement

Research in African Literatures*
Sepia Magazine
Ufahamu
Umbra

Communications Media

Africa Institute Bulletin
African Challenge
African Development
African Progress
African Urban Notes
Afrika Spectrum
Afro-American Studies
Archiv Orientální
Assegai
Ba Shiru
Beau-Cocoa
Black Arts Magazine
Black Theatre
Cricket
Ethiopian Geographical Journal
Ethiopian Observer
Freedomways
Journal of Developing Areas*

Journal of the New African Literature
  and the Arts
National Scene Magazine Supplement
Overseas Development
Presence Africaine
Race*
Review of Black Political Economy
Round Table
Rural Africana
Society of Malawi Journal
Sudan Journal of Administration and
  Development
Tropical World Review
Ufahamu
Umbra
West Africa
Zambezia

Constitutional History—See Legal and Constitutional Affairs

Cultural Affairs

AFER
Africa Institute Bulletin
Africa Magazine
Africa Today
African Affairs
African Arts*
African Challenge
African Notes

African Progress
African Scholar
African Studies
African Urban Notes
Africana Research Bulletin
Afro-American Studies
Archiv Orientální
Asia and Africa Review

Demography

TOPICAL INDEX (cont'd)

Discovery and Exploration

African Progress
Africana Marburgensia
Afrika Spectrum
Archiv Orientálni
Assegai
Beau-Cocoa
Cahiers d'Etudes Africaines
*East African Geographical
  Review*
Ethiopian Geographical Journal
Ethiopian Observer
Ethnos
*International Journal of African
  Historical Studies*
Journal of Black Studies
Journal of Ethiopian Studies
Journal of Negro History

Journal of Tropical Geography
Kleio
Nada*
Pan-African Journal
Presence Africaine
Rural Africana
*School of Oriental and African Studies
  Bulletin*
Society of Malawi Journal
Tanzania Zamani*
*Transactions of the Historical Society
  of Ghana**
Uganda
West Africa
Wiener Volkerkundliche Mitteilungen
Zambezia

Drama—*See* Theatre and Drama

Ecclesiastical Affairs—*See* Church or Ecclesiastical Affairs

Economics (including Economic History)

Africa Institute Bulletin
Africa Magazine
Africa Today
African Affairs
African Development
African Notes
African Progress
African Scholar
African Studies Review
Africana Research Bulletin
Afrika Spectrum
Afro-American Studies
*Agricultural Economics Bulletin
  for Africa*
Archiv Orientálni
Asia and Africa Review
Beau-Cocoa
Black Theatre

Cahiers d'Etudes Africaines
Civilisations*
Correspondance d'Orient Etudes
Daily News-Sunday News
East African Geographical Review*
Eastern Africa Economic Review*
Economic Bulletin of Ghana
Ethiopian Geographical Journal
Ethiopian Observer
Freedomways
*Institute for the Study of Man in
  Africa**
*Institute of Development Studies
  Bulletin**
Journal of Black Studies
Journal of Business and Social Studies
Journal of Developing Areas*
Journal of Development Studies

Education

189

Negro Educational Review
Pan-African Journal
Phylon*
Presence Africaine
Race*
Renaissance 2
Review of Black Political Economy
Rhodesian Journal of Economics
Round Table
Rural Africana
Sepia Magazine

South African Geographical Journal*
Sudan Journal of Administration and
   Development
Tropical World Review
Ufahamu
Uganda Journal
Umbra
West Africa
West African Journal of Education*
Zambezia

Ethnology

AFER
Africa
Africa Institute Bulletin
Africa Magazine
African Arts*
African Notes
African Progress
African Scholar
Africana Research Bulletin
Afro-American Studies
Archiv Orientálni
Asian and African Studies
Beau-Cocoa
Black Academy Review*
Black Theatre
Black World
Bulletin: British Association of
   Orientalists
Bulletin de la Société de
   Géographie d'Egypte
Cahiers d'Etudes Africaines
Conch
Correspondance d'Orient Etudes
East African Geographical Review
Ethiopian Observer
Ethnos
Islam
Journal of Black Studies
Journal of Ethiopian Studies

Journal of the S.W.A. Scientific Society
Lotus
Mankind Quarterly
National Scene Magazine Supplement
Pan-African Journal
Phylon*
Presence Africaine
Race*
Rocznik Orientalistyczny
Rural Africana
School of Oriental and African Studies
   Bulletin
Société des Africanistes Journal
Society of Malawi Journal
South African Archaeological Bulletin
South West African Scientific Society
   Newsletter
Studies on Developing Countries*
Sudan Journal of Administration and
   Development
Transition
Ufahamu
Uganda Journal
Umbra
West Africa
Wiener Volkerkundliche Mitteilungen
Zambezia
Zambia Museums Journal

Exploration—See Discovery and Exploration

TOPICAL INDEX (cont'd)

Film—*See* Cinema and Film

Folklore

Africa
African Arts*
African Notes
African Studies
African Studies Review
Africana Research Bulletin
Afro-American Studies
Archiv Orientálni
Asian and African Studies
Assegai
Ba Shiru
Beau-Cocoa
Black Academy Review*
Black Theatre
Black World
Bulletin: British Association of Orientalists
Cahiers d'Etudes Africaines
Conch
Ethiopian Observer
Ethnos
Folia Orientalia
Institute for the Study of Man in Africa*
Journal of Black Studies
Journal of Commonwealth Literature

Journal of Ethiopian Studies
Journal of the New African Literature and the Arts
Lotus
Nada*
National Scene Magazine Supplement
Pan-African Journal
Phylon*
Presence Africaine
Race*
Renaissance 2
Research in African Literatures*
Rocznik Orientalistyczny
School of Oriental and African Studies Bulletin
Society of Malawi Journal
Studies in Black Literature
Ufahamu
Uganda Journal
Umbra
West Africa
Wiener Volkerkundliche Mitteilungen
Zambezia
Zambia Museums Journal

Foreign Relations

Africa Institute Bulletin
Africa Magazine
Africa Today
African Affairs
African Development
African Progress
African Review*
African Scholar
African Studies Review
Afrika Spectrum
Afro-American Studies

Archiv Orientálni
Assegai
Ba Shiru
Beau-Cocoa
Black Enterprise
Black Theatre
Bulletin: British Association of Orientalists
Cahiers d'Etudes Africaines
Correspondance d'Orient Etudes
Crisis

191

Government—*See* **Politics and Government**

Historiography

African Affairs
African Challenge
African Notes
African Studies Review
African Urban Notes
Africana Marburgensia
Afrika Spectrum
Archiv Orientálni
Asian and African Studies
Black Academy Review*
Bulletin: British Association of Orientalists
Bulletin de la Société de Géographie d'Egypte
Cahiers d'Etudes Africaines
Correspondance d'Orient Etudes
Ethiopian Observer
Folia Orientalia
International Journal of African Historical Studies
Islam

Journal of Ethiopian Studies
Journal of Negro History
Kleio
Le Muséon
Pan-African Journal
Presence Africaine
Rocznik Orientalistyczny
Rural Africana
School of Oriental and African Studies Bulletin
Society of Malawi Journal
Speculum
Tanzania Zamani*
Transactions of the Historical Society of Ghana*
Ufahamu
Uganda Journal
West Africa
Zambezia

History of Education—*See* **Education**

History of Ideas

African Affairs
African Communist
African Urban Notes
Afro-American Studies
Archiv Orientálni
Asian and African Studies
Beau-Cocoa
Black Academy Review*
Black Theatre
Bulletin: British Association of Orientalists
Cahiers d'Etudes Africaines
Conch
Correspondance d'Orient Etudes

Crisis
East Africa Journal
International Journal of African Historical Studies
Islam
Journal of Ethiopian Studies
Journal of Negro History
Kleio
Lotus
Le Muséon
Muslim World
Pan-African Journal
Presence Africaine
Race*

Renaissance 2
Research in African Literatures*
Rocznik Orientalistyczny
Rural Africana
School of Oriental and African
  Studies Bulletin

Second Order
Studies in Race and Nations*
Ufahamu
Uganda Journal
Umbra
West Africa

History of Medicine—*See* Medicine (history)

International Law

See also Legal and Constitutional Affairs.

Archiv Orientálni
Comparative and International Law
  Journal of Southern Africa
Eastern Africa Law Review*
Ethiopian Observer

Howard Law Journal
Journal of Ethiopian Law*
Presence Africaine
South African Law Journal
Studies in Race and Nations*
Zambian Law Journal

International Organizations

Africa Magazine
African Affairs
African Development
African Progress
African Review*
African Scholar
African Urban Notes
Afrika Spectrum
Afro-American Studies
Archiv Orientálni
Assegai
Black Academy Review
Bulletin: British Association of
Orientalists
Comparative and International
  Law Journal of Southern Africa
Crisis
Eastern Africa Law Review*
Institute of Development Studies
  Bulletin*

Journal of Asian and African
  Studies
Journal of Commonwealth and
  Comparative Politics*
Journal of Development Studies
Journal of Negro History
Kroniek van Afrika
Pan-African Journal
Presence Africaine
Quarterly Journal of Administration
Review of Black Political Economy
Round Table
Rural Africana
Studies in Race and Nations*
Sudan Journal of Administration and
  Development
West Africa
Zambian Law Journal

International Relations—*See* Foreign Relations

Journalism—*See* Communications Media

Language

Legal and Constitutional Affairs

See also International Law, and Politics and Government.

Linguistics–*See* Language

Literature (history and criticism)

Negro American Literature Forum
Negro Educational Review
Okike
Pan-African Journal*
Phylon*
Presence Africaine
Renaissance 2
Research in African Literatures*
Rocznik Orientalistyczny
School of Oriental and African
  Studies Bulletin

South West African Scientific Society
  Newsletter
Speculum
Studies in Black Literature
Two Tone*
Ufahamu
Umbra
West Africa
World of Islam*
Zambezia

Management

Manpower and Unemployment
  Research in Africa

Maritime History

See also Naval Affairs and Transportation.

African Urban Notes
Archiv Orientálni
Bulletin: British Association of
  Orientalists
East African Geographical
  Review
Ethnos
International Journal of African
  Historical Studies

Journal of Negro History
Kleio
Presence Africaine
Rural Africana
West Africa
Zambezia

Medicine (history)

African Notes
African Progress
African Urban Notes
Afro-American Studies
Archiv Orientálni
Bulletin: British Association of
  Orientalists
Institute for the Study of Man
  in Africa*
Islam
Journal of Developing Areas*
Journal of Ethiopian Studies

Journal of Negro History
National Scene Magazine Supplement
Pan-African Journal
Presence Africaine
Rocznik Orientalistyczny
Rural Africana
School of Oriental and African
  Studies Bulletin
Society of Malawi Journal
Uganda Journal
West Africa
Zambezia

Methodology—*See* Research Methods

Military Affairs

See also Air Forces and Naval Affairs.

Africa Institute Bulletin
Africa Magazine
African Progress
African Urban Notes
Afrika Spectrum
Archiv Orientálni
Assegai
Cahiers d'Etudes Africaines
Ethiopian Observer
Journal of Developing Areas*
Journal of Ethiopian Studies
Kleio

Military History Journal
National Scene Magazine Supplement
Pan-African Journal
Presence Africaine
Round Table
Rural Africana
Society of Malawi Journal
Springbok*
Studies in Race and Nations*
Ufahamu
Uganda Journal
West Africa

Music (history)

African Arts*
African Music*
African Notes
African Progress
Africana Marburgensia
Africana Research Bulletin
Archiv Orientálni
Ba Shiru
Black Academy Review*
Black Creation
Black Theatre
Bulletin: British Association of
  Orientalists
Cahiers d'Etudes Africaines
Conch
Cricket
Ethiopian Observer
Ethnos
Forum, The
Institute for the Study of Man
  in Africa*

Islam
Journal of Ethiopian Studies
Journal of Negro History
Journal of the New African Literature
  and the Arts
Lotus
Nada*
Pan-African Journal
Presence Africaine
Renaissance 2
School of Oriental and African
  Studies Bulletin
Société des Africanistes Journal
Society of Malawi Journal
Speculum
Uganda Journal
Umbra
West Africa

Lotus
Pan-African Journal
Presence Africaine
School of Oriental and African
  Studies Bulletin

Second Order
Speculum
West Africa

Political Science—*See* Politics and Government

Politics and Government

Africa Institute Bulletin
Africa Magazine
Africa Today
African Affairs
African Communist
African Development
African Notes
African Progress
African Review*
African Scholar
African Studies
African Studies Review
African Urban Notes
Africana Research Bulletin
Afrika Spectrum
Afro-American Studies
Archiv Orientálni
Asia and Africa Review
Asian and African Studies
Ba Shiru
Black Enterprise
Black Theatre
Black World
Bulletin: British Association of
  Orientalists
Cahiers d'Etudes Africaines
Civilisations*
Correspondance d'Orient Etudes
Crisis
Daily News—Sunday News
East Africa Journal
Freedomways
Howard Law Journal
Institute of Development
  Studies Bulletin*

International Journal of African
  Historical Studies
Journal of Black Studies
Journal of Business and Social
  Studies
Journal of Commonwealth and
  Comparative Politics
Journal of Developing Areas*
Journal of Development Studies
Journal of Ethiopian Studies
Journal of Modern African Studies
Kleio
Kroniek van Afrika
Legon Observer
Lotus
Manpower and Unemployment Research
  in Africa
National Scene Magazine Supplement
Negro American Literature Forum
Overseas Development
Pan-African Journal
Presence Africaine
Quarterly Journal of Administration
Race*
Renaissance 2
Review of Black Political Economy
Rhodesia and World Report
Round Table
Rural Africana
Sepia Magazine
Studies in Race and Nations*
Studies on Developing Countries*
Sudan Journal of Administration and
  Development
Transition

Tropical World Review
Ufahamu
World of Islam*

Zambezia
Zambian Law Journal
Zimbabwe News

Population—*See* Demography

Public Administration—*See* Politics and Government

Religious Studies (non-denominational, non-institutional)

See also Church or Ecclesiastical Affairs.

AFER
Africa
Africa Institute Bulletin
African Challenge
African Notes
African Scholar
African Studies Review
Africana Marburgensia
Afro-American Studies
Archiv Orientálni
Asian and African Studies
Black Academy Review*
Black Theatre
Bulletin: British Association of
  Orientalists
Correspondance d'Orient Etudes
Institute for the Study of Man
  in Africa*
Islam
Journal of Ethiopian Studies

Journal of Religion in Africa
Lotus
Le Muséon
National Scene Magazine Supplement
Orita*
Presence Africaine
Renaissance 2
Rocznik Orientalistyczny
School of Oriental and African
  Studies Bulletin
Second Order
Société des Africanistes Journal
Society of Malawi Journal
Ufahamu
Uganda Journal
Wiener Volkerkundliche Mitteilungen
World of Islam*
Zambezia

Research Methods

Africa Magazine
African Notes
African Urban Notes
Africana Marburgensia
Afrika Spectrum
Archiv Orientálni
Black Theatre
Conch

Eastern Africa Law Review*
East African Geographical Review
Ethnos
Ghana Journal of Education
Institute of Development Studies
  Bulletin*
International Journal of African
  Historical Studies

201

Journal of Asian and African
  Studies
Journal of Developing Areas*
Kleio
Manpower and Unemployment
  Research in Africa
Negro Educational Review
Overseas Development
Pan-African Journal
Presence Africaine
Quarterly Journal of Administration
Race*

Research in African Literatures*
Review of Black Political Economy
Rural Africana
South African Archaeological Bulletin
Studies in Race and Nations*
Sudan Journal of Administration and
  Development
West African Journal of Archaeology
Wiener Volkerkundliche Mitteilungen
Zambezia
Zambia Museums Journal

Science and Technology

Africa Magazine
African Development
African Progress
African Studies Review
African Urban Notes
Afro-American Studies
Black Theatre
Conch
Ethnos
Institute of Development
  Studies Bulletin*
International Journal of African
  Historical Studies
Journal of Developing Areas*

Journal of Modern African Studies
Manpower and Unemployment Research
  in Africa
National Scene Magazine Supplement
Overseas Development
Presence Africaine
Review of Black Political Economy
Rural Africana
Society of Malawi Journal
Speculum
Sudan Journal of Administration and
  Development
West Africa

Social History

Africa
Africa Institute Bulletin
Africa Today
African Affairs
African Communist
African Notes
African Progress
African Scholar
African Studies Review
African Urban Notes
Africana Research Bulletin
Afro-American Studies
Archiv Orientálni

Asian and African Studies
Black Academy Review*
Black Theatre
Black World
Bulletin: British Association of
  Orientalists
Bulletin de la Société de
  Géographie d'Egypte
Cahiers d'Etudes Africaines
Civilisations*
Correspondance d'Orient Etudes
Crisis
Ethiopian Observer

202

Sociology

Manpower and Unemployment
  Research in Africa
Muslim World
Nada*
Negro Educational Review
Overseas Development
Pan-African Journal
Phylon*
Presence Africaine
Race*
Race Relations News
Renaissance 2
Rural Africana

Second Order
Sepia Magazine
Société des Africanistes Journal
Studies in Race and Nations*
Studies on Developing Countries*
Survey of Race Relations in South
  Africa
Tropical World Review*
Ufahamu
Uganda Journal
West Africa
Zambia Museums Journal
Zambian Urban Studies

Technology—See Science and Technology

Theatre and Drama

See also Cinema and Film.

African Arts*
African Music*
African Notes
African Studies Review
Archiv Orientálni
Asia and African Review
Asian and African Studies
Ba Shiru
Beau-Cocoa
Black Academy Review*
Black Arts Magazine
Bulletin: British Association of
  Orientalists
Cahiers d'Etudes Africaines
Conch
Cricket
Crisis
Daily News-Sunday News
English Studies in Africa

Freedomways
Journal of Commonwealth Literature
Journal of the New African Literature
  and the Arts
Literature East and West
Lotus
National Scene Magazine Supplement
Negro American Literature Forum
Presence Africaine
Research in African Literatures*
Rocznik Orientalistyczny
School of Oriental and African Studies
  Bulletin
Sepia Magazine
Studies in Black Literature
Ufahamu
Umbra
West Africa
Zambezia

TOPICAL INDEX (cont'd)

Transportation

African Challenge
African Development
African Progress
African Urban Notes
Africana Research Bulletin
Afrika Spectrum
Archiv Orientálni
*Bulletin de la Société de
  Géographie d'Egypte*
Daily News-Sunday News
East African Geographical Review
Journal of Developing Areas*

Journal of Tropical Geography
Kleio
*Manpower and Unemployment
  Research in Africa*
Overseas Development
Presence Africaine
Rural Africana
South African Geographical Journal*
*Sudan Journal of Administration and
  Development*
West Africa
Zambezia

Unspecified

*Annual Report of the South
  African Institute of Race
  Relations**